Printed in the United States of America
ISBN: 978-1495939983

Novus Venalicium, Inc.
4742 Liberty Rd S #262
Salem, OR 97302
503-339-6000

TABLE OF
CONTENTS

Preface 3

Introduction 4

Chapter 1
  A Changing Industry 31

Chapter 2
  Two Types of Marketing 39

Chapter 3
  How to Stand Out & Capture More of
  Your Market 43

Chapter 4
  The Most Important Position in
  Your Dental Office 47

Chapter 5
  A Checklist for Successful Ads 53

Chapter 6
  The Best, Most Cost-Effective, Source for
  New Patients 61

    Internal Marketing 62

      Newsletter, Postcards/Direct Mail 62

      Signage 62

      Buttons 62

      Conversation/Suggestion 63

Excitement 63

Events.. 64

Reactivation 64

Referral contests 65

Recognition..................................... 65

Video/Documentary 66

Referrals from other sources 66

Social Media.................................... 66

Chapter 7

Going Outside: External Marketing to
Attract New Patients........................ 69

External Marketing.......................... 70

Direct Mail 70

Newspapers/Print Media................ 71

Yellow Pages.................................... 72

Web (+ email follow-up)................. 73

Radio.. 73

Gum Shoe Marketing 74

Press.. 74

Book Authorship 75

Seminars/Speaking......................... 75

Other People's Lists 76

Management of Marketing 76

Inter-Vergence Marketing 76

Infusionsoft.................................... 78

People 78

Results/Is it paying? 79

Who/expertise 80

Dental Insurance 81

Chapter 8

Successful Management of a Dental Practice in a
PPO Environment 83

Chapter 9

The 33 Trooths about Advertising for Dentists 93

Chapter 10

Write a Book and Become a Celebrity 99

Chapter 11

How to Clone Yourself in Your Marketing 105

Chapter 12

How a Small-Town Dentist in Rural America
Generated 549 New Patients From a
Three-Hour Event Without Any Marketing! 111

Chapter 13

The Internet from 50,000 Feet 123

Internet Marketing Sales Reps Are
~~Honest~~ People 124

"You can't track that!" 124

Social Media Marketing Is A Lie 125

Critical Error: Using more than one company. ... 126

There Are Only Two, True Options 127

Getting Your Website to Rank is ONLY
10% of the work 127

Get people to stay on your site! 129

Keep It Fresh. 129

Getting people to visit your website. 130

Customer Reviews 131

Paying For Website Visitors 134

    Google Ads 135

    Facebook Ads 135

    Bing/Yahoo Ads 135

    Yelp Ads 135

    Retargeting.. 136

    Banner Ads.. 136

    Yodle and Reach Local........................... 136

Chapter 14

The Secret to Getting New Referrals..................... 139

Why Is This More Important Today? 143

Here's Game Changer #1: 144

Moving On To Game Changer #2:...................... 145

Bringing Us to Game Changer #3:...................... 147

Wrapping Up With Game Changer #4: 147

What Does This Mean To You? 152

What Is Your Local Online Reputation?............. 153

What's Next?.. 154

Chapter 15

You Can Laugh At Not Getting New
Patients...If You Follow This Simple Plan.............157

What Is Reputation Marketing? 158

How Do You Create A Reputation
Marketing Strategy? 159

Step 1: Build Your Reputation 160

Step 2: Market Your Reputation 163

Step 3: Manage Your Reputation 166

Step 4: Create Your Culture 168

Putting It All Together 169

Chapter 16

Applying Your Powers of Social Proof 173

What are patient testimonials? 177

Types of Patient Video Testimonials 184

#1 - The Delivered Testimonial 184

#2 - The Interview Testimonial 188

But what questions do you ask a patient? 191

How do you get patient testimonials? 191

How to leverage your video
social proof in your practice 196

The Fastest Path to Case Acceptance
(the cash) 200

Chapter 17

Implementation 215

Disclaimer

Publisher: Novus Venalicium, Inc.
Cover Design: MegaBucks Marketing
Production & Composition: Novus Venalicium, Inc.

This publication is designed to provide accurate and authoritative information in regard to the subject matter covered. It is sold with the understanding that the publisher is not engaged in rendering legal, accounting or other professional services. If legal advice or other expert assistance is required, the services of a competent professional should be sought.

The primary author, Jerry A. Jones, and his companies,

do not represent nor have any formal business relationships with the co-authors of this book. By purchasing or reading this book, the Reader agrees that any actions taken or not taken as a result of reading this book, on his or her behalf, is done so after conducting their own due diligence with the author or co-author of this book and that any such action is the Reader's responsibility. Neither the author nor other co-authors may be held liable for any action or lack of taken on behalf of the Reader.

Jones, Jerry A., 1972 –
The definitive guide to dental practice success: time tested secrets to attract new patients & retain your existing patients /by Jerry A. Jones & 8 Other contributors

Printed in the United States of America

**TIME-TESTED SECRETS TO ATTRACT NEW
& RETAIN EXISTING PATIENTS**

Preface

This preface is provided to get the reader to focus, front and center, on what's *really* happening in Dentistry today. Not theory. Not hype. Not scare tactics. Just business reality.

The following pages in this preface and subsequent introduction appeared in my first-ever publicly released perspective on the dental industry titled, *The State of Dentistry & Its Unstoppable Evolution: 7 Startling Discoveries & Shocking Truths*. To learn more about the State of Dentistry and receive relevant, new insights, optin at **TheStateOfDentistry.com**.

The purpose of first reviewing the State of Dentistry is to identify key change points in the dental industry evolution beyond 2014 and thru 2023, and what solo GPs must do to adapt, survive and profit.

Introduction

The following, *The State of Dentistry & Its Unstoppable Evolution...*, is for the solo GP or the new graduate who might be a future solo GP that wants to be ahead of the sea change occurring *right now* in Dentistry. If you are at all thin-skinned or easily offended by economic realities and truths, proceed at your own risk.

If, on the other hand, you want to grab the future by the horns and will it, even command it, to serve your needs, the following exposé will be of enormous benefit to you.

Without question, the new economy is finicky. It requires different input from us, as its willing participants, to get the same output as before. The discoveries and truths revealed in the following pages are specifically written to prepare you for a time of renewed prosperity and to set you up to profit as the dental industry twists, turns, bends and, in many places as you'll soon see, breaks.

When I finally decided it was time to put down, in words and on paper, what I see happening after twenty years in Dentistry, I was tempted not to refer to this as a "State of the Industry" paper, but instead, I initially wanted to call it, "Seven Startling Realities & Truths Making Rich Dentists Even Richer."

Why such a name? Because, I see, talk to and correspond with a number of high-net-worth Dentists all over the U.S. Many of them are also Members of my Clear Path Society® or franchisees of my Wellness Springs Dental® (info @ www.WellnessSpringsDental.com.) From the private client work I do with them including marketing and business growth strategies, I know who is doing well and who is struggling and why. I know that in many different cities and states some are still reeling from the economic chaos birthed in the early 2000s, while others are quietly making significant incomes, fortunes even, in Dentistry.

Three of my top Members immediately come to mind. They're each earning in excess of $1,000,000 annually from their practices. Yes, *even in this economy.*

I also have my own business experiences and dental office to draw from. This, in addition to the information I gain from my members and visible trends in the industry, is how I derived the seven core relevant areas listed below, and more importantly, how they will affect the future of the solo general practitioner dentist (GP).

My dental office, Wellness Springs Dental® of Salem, Oregon, is a mid-sized dental office with four doctors. It was born before the crash of '08 (in late 2004) and, before, during and now, is continually growing outpacing any non-chain-owned dental practice in the area. Incidentally, many refer to these chains as the face of "Corporate Dentistry." Since most Dentists own corporations, I think the label is inaccurate and misleading.

Combine my twenty years in Dentistry (where I've worked with some of the most noted "experts," gurus and thought-leaders), a decade of developing a concept dental office from scratch, and turning it into a substantial local business doing well in excess of 7 figures annually, and you will find what I found: the discoveries inside this report are not only coming to light, but fruition as well.

I speak from experience, not from an Ivory Tower. I am not someone who merely "consults" with dentists; I'm in the trenches, not as a dentist, mind you, but as an owner of a dental office and as someone working one-on-one with well over a hundred of my Clear Path Society® Members and Private Clients...*Right now*. I've taken my share of lumps. Still, I've survived and done very well...for over twenty years in this industry.

For much of those two decades, I've quietly worked with my Members and private clients, built up my own dental office, started and sold a private school, and more (I've created, started and/or sold over fourteen different businesses).

Like it or not, excited or not, know this: if you want to survive *and* financially benefit from the coming changes in our industry, you must be aware of and understand the macro view – the bigger picture of what's coming and what's already happening from the standpoint of a business owner...not just a clinical dentist.

If you are stubbornly only wearing the "clinical dentist" hat and not the "businessman" hat you may well find yourself punching a clock for a group practice or some other chain - not necessarily bad, but certainly leaving you with an undefined future. Unless you take immediate steps to become a part of this impending inevitable industry disruption, rather than fighting it, it is a future over which you will have little say.

This report, now, as preface of this book, consists of seven core areas, not necessarily in any particular order of importance:

- The New Economy & Practice/Business Overhead
- The New Economy & Practice Management
- The New Economy & Marketing
- The New Economy & Consolidation
- The New Economy & Technology
- The New Economy & Financing
- The New Economy & Non-Dentist Innovation & Ownership

There is a major disruption coming, *similar to* what happened in medicine – when MDs went from making $1/2- to $3/4-million a year to $1/4-million or less virtually overnight. No one cries for them, but there is a reason why we have a shortage of physicians, and given the new healthcare act, medical student enrollment certainly will not be helped.

With disruption and chaos comes opportunity. It will be available for you, should you want it *and* recognize it.

Because it's most likely on your mind (or should be), I decided to start my analysis with what I've discovered about Dental Office Overhead in this, the new economy...

Overhead

Has your overhead increased or decreased in the last twelve to twenty-four months? Do you know for sure by how much? Have you offset the increases? Or, have you just eaten them in hopes they'll go away, so you can "keep your fees down?"

Staffing costs continue to soar. Payroll taxes alone are crippling many small businesses, particularly dental offices.
Simple office supplies (even a lowly ream of paper) have jumped dramatically in price.

Rents are not decreasing in the vast majority of towns and cities. Moreover, if you want to own or build, both existing building prices and new construction prices are setting records. Furthermore, despite the economic malaise, there is no hope of a decrease in either, any time soon. Adding expense to constructing your own site are the myriad codes that must be met in any new building...from OSHA to structural and engineering, the ADA (American's with Disabilities Act), and more.

Without question, it's becoming more and more difficult to keep everyday expenses under control.

Let's not forget how our local, state and federal governments continue to add layer upon layer of bureaucracy to our businesses, upping the number of forms we're "required by law" to take time to fill out and return, additional fees to be paid, taxes levied, etc.

It is a daily fight to keep overhead under control and keep our dental offices functioning. This overhead "creep," while virtually invisible as it is happening, by year-end is immediately evident.

There are only four ways to combat increased overhead:

- Increase fees;
- Increase production;
- Decrease expenses; and/or
- Become more efficient.

I advise my Members, private clients, and my own office, Wellness Springs Dental® of Salem, to ALWAYS focus on all four ways. One and two are easy. Three is a little more difficult (limit debt and financed purchases!)And four, we must look for outside help from folks like Dr. Chris Griffin*, the most efficient man in dentistry.

If you can't make tough decisions and get your overhead under control so you're profitable, don't worry, someone else may be along soon to help.

However, their help won't be your idea of being helped; they'll be helping themselves to a broken practice for pennies on the dollar. Deep in debt, burned out, and disgusted with dentistry, you'll be ready and willing to give it all up.

Management

For years in dentistry, we've accepted and operated under the guise that a dentist could easily have, as a solo practitioner, a profitable office with one front office person, two dental assistants and one hygienist, all neatly packaged into a 1,500 square foot, three-operatory office.

That reality has changed.

Unless you're in a unique situation, making money in the above setting beyond 2014 is going to become incredibly difficult and stressful, if not impossible.

The limitations on capacity for solo GPs become quickly evident.

There are a small number of practitioners who will do just fine in this case. However, they'll be niched, they'll be forced to become savvy marketers and, worse, they'll be left to manage their practice themselves, while continuing to practice dentistry only three to four days per week.

The facility, the investment the GP has made into staffing his or her office, will sit idle the other 3 to 4 days every week.

The lost income and opportunities are enormous. *This is happening all over.*

Did I just describe you?

As an investor, would YOU invest in a business that had excess capacity that wasn't being used? Nope, you'd dump it in a hot second.

This is where management comes into play. For a solo dentist to thrive and profit beyond 2014, you'll be required to have a single person focused on the management of and maximizing the return on investment for every aspect of the office including patient scheduling, use of the physical plant, insurance reimbursements, legal and OSHA compliance, marketing, patient re-care/recall, and more.

There's barely enough time to stay current on clinical CE requirements and keep up with the management of the practice. Moreover, that conflict will continue to strengthen the argument that even small offices of three or four ops and a half-dozen staff needs management help. Your Fridays, when the office is closed, will soon become absorbed with paperwork and non-income producing activities that hit your bottom line with a huge blob of red ink.

A transition here must take place. You as clinician, manager and owner must become leader and clinician, *delegating* the management responsibilities.

At Wellness Springs Dental® of Salem, we've invested heavily in having a competent on-site office manager/COO (Chief Operations Officer) that is both knowledgeable in clinical dentistry <u>and</u> what it takes to run an effective, efficient, productive and profitable office.

I've referred a number of my clients to one of my top Clear Path Society® Members, Dr. Sean Tarpenning's* office in Eau Claire, WI. His top-flight office manager and support staff are an exemplary example of how a modern office should be managed.

Unless you allow your practice to be staffed, ran and managed *like the business it is*, you'll never prosper in this new, ruthless economy. No longer is good management and good staffing enough. It must be spot-on or you'll keep writing checks to cover shortfalls and you won't even know why.

If you think you can do it all yourself, again, someone will be along soon to help. However, it won't be the beneficial help you can get now by installing a professional to truly manage your business.

Marketing

For a solo GP to survive and profit beyond 2014, marketing must become a major focus. The generation of new patients becomes more important than ever. People move more. Loyalty is out the window. It's all about, "What have you done for me, *today?*"

The vast majority of GPs, while focusing on new patient generation, ignore their greatest asset: existing patients. It's no wonder why 7% to 10% of your practice disappears annually – due mostly to perceived neglect or total indifference. Either way, the effect on your practice is the same.

If you are not constantly making significant increases and building your patient base, it IS eroding. Often dentists find, to their surprise, when they sell (or when they buy), they have far fewer "active" patients than they thought. For the record, active patients, for me, means they have a "next" appointment. If they don't, they're as good as gone)!

To make matters more complicated, dental marketing has continued to evolve at the hands of "progressive" media.

Until about 2008, you could rely on the Big '5' for new patients: insurance plans, Yellow Pages, newspaper, radio and direct mail (and, of course, word-of-mouth).

Of course, that was back when a $1500 maximum reimbursement for a patient with insurance actually meant they could get significant work done. Now it's barely enough for two exams each year, a couple of cleanings and, at most, two or three fillings (or, no exams, etc., and just a crown).

Aggressive marketers used to be able to generate a 3% response or more from a single, simple, inexpensive postcard mailing to almost any given area.

Today, marketers have to contend with: social media, everything Internet (search engine optimization, reputation control/defender, YouTube, Google, Bing, Yahoo!, websites, directories, Angie's List, and so on), event marketing, in-and-out-of office seminars, insurance plans, Yellow Pages, specialized newspapers, radio and direct mail.

Many have said that Yellow Pages are dying. In some areas, yes, they are. However, it's a painfully slow death. In many rural areas, my Members and private clients are still having solid success from remaining IN the Yellow Pages. Even in a moderately sized town (Salem, Oregon), with 120,000+ residents, we do very well being in the Yellow Pages directories. One of our primary audiences *still* regularly relies on them as a directory or *where to go and who to call: the 55+ pre-retired, retired seniors and boomers.*

You should not need my own experiences or those of my Members and private clients to tell you that not having a properly promoted and positioned website is a major error.

The vast majority (95+% or more) of dental websites I've reviewed, including those put out by the big dental website promoters, lack fundamentals to make them search engine friendly, so they don't appear at the very top (as in top 3) of the "organic" listings. Bottom line: If you're not on page one of a Google search for "City, State Dentist," you're missing massive amounts of free traffic and a free source of new patients. You also miss the opportunity to list-build by capturing visitors that opt-in to receiving valuable information from the office.

The Internet is also a place where disgruntled patients and staff can post anonymous, damaging complaints about you and your services (and staff). In today's "it's not my fault" world, you have to be on guard and police the Internet for slanderous material that affects how others perceive your reputation. This is a very real, problematic issue that must be monitored, reviewed and dealt with regularly.

In recent discoveries from my own marketing efforts, and on behalf of my Members and private clients, we're continuing to make direct response mail pay off very well. The US Postal Service's problematic changes – closures, reduced hours, days and so on – were nullified, in my opinion, with their introduction of EDDM, or, Every Door Direct Mail. Right now, utilizing this service provides us one of the most solid ROIs in direct mail, for my Members, my private clients and myself.

Newspapers, while dying a similar slow death like yellow page directories, also still have incredibly useful distribution and allow for inexpensive promotion, if you know how to approach them. At Wellness Springs Dental® of Salem, we're in the newspaper every month. Moreover, every month, we're peeling a solid twenty to thirty new patients from that source.

If you are not regularly mailing to your existing patients, you're missing out on an important opportunity to educate, retain, train to refer, and entertain (don't underestimate the importance of this). Many dentists erroneously believe that email is a solid substitute for mailing a hard-copy newsletter, paper and ink, to their patients.

While a good *addition to*, emailed newsletters are nowhere near as valuable, nor is there a proper substitute for a real printed newsletter. Emails in and of themselves, by nature, have no value. Printed materials, such as this paper in fact, have tremendous perceived and actual value to the recipients.

I recognize a number of my private clients and Members, in particular Dr. Scott Westermeier

- a dentist turned expert marketer of implants
- as an example of taking New Economy opportunities and using them to generate a

sizeable personal net income bumping up close to or in excess of $1,000,000 annually.

Changing "one thing" in his marketing plan has resulted in his office producing, with three doctors, $6+ million in 2013 alone. Yes... three doctors. Interestingly enough, *his story is not unique.* There are dozens more like this – some even more mind-boggling.

Incidentally, the chief reason I started the Membership program I've written about above, The Clear Path Society®, was to help Dentists employ proven strategies and techniques to market their practice, control their overhead and continue to explore new practice opportunities.

Consolidation

In a desperate email, a former client contacted me recently, exasperated about a national chain building a brand-new, state-of-the-art office two doors down from him, on a desirable corner in his little northwest town.

He had his chance to "own" the corner. He had his chance to be the biggest multi-doctor office in his town. Back in the day, the Dentist-Brotherhood would sort of respect that. Today, there's no such thing. Chain dentistry doesn't care about what might have been and <u>neither should you</u>. The good 'ol days and good 'ol boys are all retired.

It's time to move forward.

I did indicate he had some hope, but I was frank when I explained it was going to require substantial investment on his part to maintain his position and, in fact, he would require even larger investment if he wanted continue to make money in his market.

National chains are likely coming to your town, if they're not there already. You'll either be fighting for the same new patients as they are (they've deeper pockets and they will win), join them as an associate or "part owner" or, you'll establish yourself in the community as everything *they are not*. The latter, unless you're interested in a sell and merge situation, is certainly the master key to surviving chain dentistry.

Given the non-stop increases in overhead, consolidating practices with another dentist or specialist enables you to harness the power of shared overhead.

At Wellness Springs Dental® of Salem, we have ten doctor days of dentistry Monday-Friday. We have two doctors working simultaneously, sharing all the expenses - effectively splitting them in half. Consolidation is a simple, highly effective concept. *It's a no-brainer.*

I firmly believe that in another five to ten years, we'll regularly begin to see dentists as part of hospital or urgent care staff. (Maybe hospitals will get into the dental market, and if they do, watch out. They have *insanely* deep pockets and could easily drive government-subsidized dental offices to close their doors. I'm doing my best to make inroads, but it's a stubborn path. They *are* busy.)

You'll also begin to see non-dentist owned offices popping up. (Just Google "MSO" and "DSO" – Management Service Organization and Dental Service Organization.) They'll offer all the same services you do, but with expanded hours, shared overhead, and a nationally-recognized franchise run by businesspeople who understand both the mechanics of profitable business and the unique dynamics of dentistry. (This is the reality of my franchise, Wellness Springs Dental®)

With graduates from dental school weighed down with a hundred thousand or more in student loan debt (some at $200,000+), needing to go to work NOW to repay their loans and, with almost half of graduating classes being women, national chains and large groups are the ideal setting for them. Chains and groups often require no initial investment and they provide mentoring and training – both of which are big on a graduate's list of requirements for employment. I know, I talk to new graduates constantly and have interviewed close to fifty or sixty for positions at my own office. Because going further into debt to open a solo practice is risky, it's less likely a future proposition for the vast majority of graduates.

New graduates are looking for places where they can go to work the same day, have no personal overhead and, more importantly, no risk or responsibility beyond the clinical practice of dentistry.

Were I a solo GP, I'd be looking for partnerships with other dentists to create reputable, reliable group practices or, adding associates as fast as I could find them, to take advantage of the coming sea change in dentistry.

Your choices will be limited, as solo GPs will continue to struggle to exist *beyond* 2014. Moreover, as I dig a little deeper into this exposé, you'll see why.

Technology

The great news about dentistry is this: technology is evolving so quickly that, for example, in less than a decade, it's very possible that virtually every dental office will be using digital impression scanners and manufacturing their own crowns, aligner trays and any oral appliance currently manufactured in a lab setting now right in their own office.

This doesn't bode well for the lab business. It's an evolutionary, disruptive change, I'd be willing to bet that one or two labs are at the forefront of this change right now.

3-D printers (like the CEREC, E4D, etc.) will become as common in a dental office as digital x-rays. They will also, at some point, be reasonably priced. In the meantime, CAD-CAM, 3-D digital impression and x-ray technologies generally require massive capital investments.

In a recent, candid conversation with dental lab owner, David Block, CDT, of Aesthetic Porcelain Studios, he shared much of the same thoughts I have on clinical technology and how it will change the landscape of Dentistry and the industries associated with Dentistry, like the lab business, in the very near future.

With the exception of one, every dentist I know that has these technologies has borrowed from the bank to get it. At an enormous cost. Few pay cash. Few can afford to. And, therein lies the issue.

Their fixed overheads are actually higher (not good for economic downturns – they're stuck making that payment no matter what). They may be more efficient. But one of the principles of a practice that profits and thrives beyond 2014 will be one that is totally debt-free, owes no bank or note holder of any kind, and has free cash flow of 15%-20% or greater of their current monthly income. That's 80% to 85% overhead MAXIMUM with doctor pay included!

If you or your practice owes money, you are restricting your freedom of choice and only working for someone else. They hold the cards. They hold you hostage until you've paid them off...in full.

Technology is great. However, the solo doc that embarks on purchasing it all should beware. Debt is yet another strong consideration for group practices when looking at new technology and a force that solo GPs will compete with when the big dental practice chains come to town.

There is a time to buy and a time to sit on the sidelines.

Cash is king. If you owe anyone, they own you. Get out of all debt as fast as you can.

Financing

There are two rules to live by in the world of financing for a solo GP's survival beyond 2014:

1.) You'll need to learn how to manage financing activities for your patients actively. If you want to do more treatment more often and keep your fees where they should be, you'll need to embrace in-office financing. There's a way to do it that mitigates risk and keeps you under the national average of bad-debt write-offs by companies large and small. At my office, we manage our accounts receivable portfolio in a very professional manner. It's responsible for earning us thousands of dollars in interest every month that more than offsets the bad debt write-offs we occasionally experience from the act of extending credit.

Understand why Care Credit® and other companies are happy to have your best patients financed through them while you take a 10% (or more) discount hit when they pay you upfront: It's HUGELY profitable for them.

There is, however, a time when you should and shouldn't finance patients. Moreover, there is a time when a 10% discount means more than 18% interest. It's all about cash flow and how strong it is. This is a deciding factor for most. However, if you're debt-free and have a healthy regular monthly cash flow, you must consider financing your patients.

2.) Unless you are financing a patient, you should not be involved in financing yourself. This simply means that unless you can afford to pay cash, today, you must not make the purchase. ANY purchase. Go back to the days of our grandparents and parents and embrace the principle of delayed gratification.

I'm fond of thinking and saying, "Frugal is the new black." It's not being "cheap," it's being smart.

However, be careful not to confuse "frugal and intelligent buying decisions" with being "cheap." I wholeheartedly buy into the concept and thought process of *abundance*. I do believe there are limitless opportunities and an income limited only by your imagination to help others achieve what they want so that you may achieve your own goals (credit to Zig Ziglar).

You should also understand the concept of value. Price is what you pay. Value is what you get. Rare is it in our world today where price and value are equally represented. Value is not big in the world of discount retailers. Instead, they live and die by price. You should not. You should embrace value. *You should be on the constant lookout for opportunities to make investments in yourself and in your practice that enhance the value you deliver to patients.*

I hear from far too many doctors that are concerned about "being sold" something vs. taking what are incredible resources and utilizing them to their fullest.

If you fear investing in both yourself and your business, with a focus on how quickly you can generate *yet another positive ROI*, you will be poverty-laden, weighed down by emotional baggage that is counter-productive to hitting or exceeding the smallest financial goals.

A mindset rooted in poverty and a "limited size of pie" (as in, there's only so much pie – I want my piece and that's all I get) will keep you right where you are.

Non-Dentist Involvement

I alluded to this earlier: be ready to accept and understand why non-dentists will be getting into and taking ownership, or at the very least, operational control of the non-clinical aspects of dental offices.

In most states, a non-dentist cannot own a dental "practice." There are some that allow it (Arizona is one). Here in Oregon, where I reside, non-dentists cannot own a practice. However, a practice is defined as the "patient charts."

That leaves a lot of latitude for non-dentists to own everything but the charts, with the chart ownership relegated to a clinical director or a partner in the entity with the non-dentist. There are many ways to achieve this. The most popular is integrating the MSO/DSO practice model.

An evolution is underway in Dentistry. Chains will continue to pop-up and prosper, and I have started the process of launching a national dental office franchise, a *real* franchise, which will be available for purchase and operation by both Dentists and non-dentists, depending on their state of operation and a number of other factors. (Note: This is not an offer to sell a franchise location to you.)

This could well be a threat to your future. In fact, I'd be more nervous of a real franchise entering the industry than I would of yet another "chain" with the same old premise and promise to its stakeholders and doctors.

Why?

Dentistry can be highly profitable. It's a clean industry. It's simple to understand and it's relatively recession-proof since everyone will most likely need a dentist at some point if they truly value their health.

All of the above attracts business people. There are few industries that, when properly managed, can crank out a reliable 15%-20% net profit once there is a sufficient volume of dentistry being completed every month. More importantly, once synergy exists between the two parties – dentists and practice managers – profits will increase.

In no way should you construe my comments as a businessman or woman having an influence or impact on the clinical care of patients. To me and in my organization, there is always a very black, heavy line between the two areas. Dentists must always control clinical care.

As a solo GP, you'll need to go from actually doing the dentistry to managing your staff, being a leader, and being an investor into your own business. Essentially you will need to function in more than just the clinical role, if you are to be successful beyond right now.

A businessperson can come into this profession, study it for a year or less, understand what makes things run and without having to learn one single thing about clinical dentistry, have an office up and open right next door to you, without ever spending one single second in dental school.

Analysis, Conclusion, Important Notes & WHAT TO DO NEXT

After reading what I have outlined on the future of the industry (I've grown to love), some will get nervous. Scared even.

You shouldn't be scared. *However, you should be
concerned* about your future in dentistry if you are a
solo GP and about your ability to care for your family
by earning an extraordinary income that will allow you
to experience a future of freedom.

Smart, forward-thinkers will sense these massive
changes, as I do, and see them as tremendous
opportunities in an industry that is positioned for an
incredible disturbance.

Remember, these aren't mere theories from a
disconnected, uninitiated Ph.D., an uninformed,
tuned-out academic, or government bureaucrat. This is
reality – these shifts are in motion now. I see them
occurring and developing as I write this. The
groundwork has been laid, the foundations poured,
walls going up, and trusses ordered. Rooftops are
arriving soon.

Either you'll become a "victim" or you'll understand all
this and arrange now to situate your own practice to
prosper greatly.

It's your call. Moreover, time is not on your side.

*Much of what I've discussed and outlined here won't
be something you can pull off by yourself.*

Those that try may just fail. Aligning with the wrong
parties could result in failure, too, ultimately.

Like having an office manager to "manage" the
hundreds of moving parts – employees, vendors,
insurance companies, government agencies, *patients,*

etc. – you're going to need experts operating successfully inside the dental industry who can point to *their* current successes and say, "We can do the same thing for you. Here's why and here's how. And, we guarantee your satisfaction."

Without help, pulling off survival beyond 2014 is going to be difficult. Having reliable, ethical partners invested in your success is a proven formula for getting you where you want to go. Again, you don't need "theorists" pontificating about our industry. You need actual experts who live, and breathe, even while on vacation, their passions.

Dear Reader...You have this book in your hands at the right time. Whether you decide to remain a solo practitioner, go "group" or open a franchised dental office, this book will help you reach the pinnacle of success that you've defined.

It will help you create a future *you control*. A future that permits complete and total freedom. Breaking you away from every chain that's holding you back.

You'll achieve all this through expanding your knowledge, shifting your mindset and seeing what IS possible. You'll see and witness first hand, what *other doctors, just like you, are doing right now that has changed their current and future economic reality.*

It applies to you, too. And, all this can happen in short order. I don't mean next year or next decade, *but right now*. In your office.

*These individuals presented at my 2013 seminar, Dental Office: IMPOSSIBLE. Some have also contributed to this book.

Information at www.DentalOfficeImpossible.com

Chapter 1

A Changing Industry

If there's ever been a time in dentistry when a dental success guidebook is mandatory to grow a practice, about what to do, with whom and when, that time is now. Dentists all over are facing more and more pressure to do more for less.

Changes are taking shape throughout the industry at every level. Everything is being turned on its proverbial head, from dental labs and other necessary service providers to the technology and way you promote your practice.

Almost nothing is as it was two, three, five or ten years ago. The industry is undergoing massive change at lightning speed, and dentists are struggling to keep up.

There are, however, tenets of business that have not changed and will never change. There are also aspects of marketing and building relationships that are time-tested and, until human psychology morphs, these too, will remain constants.

There are several challenges that many dentists struggle with.

   1.) *Integrating the changes* in technology and in the business environment with these psychological constants;

   2.) *Implementing the changes*; and,

   3.) *Accountability*. Is what you're doing really making money? Or, is it our worst money fear: a total and utter waste?

This book is a manual that details how to succeed in the business of dentistry right now and into the future. It will guide you to an understanding of these changes, help you adapt to them, and show you how to prevent being passed over, left to struggle, or worse, broke and wondering what happened to all the patients you used to treat.

If you want to succeed in Dentistry, or any business for that matter, you have to understand, with absolute clarity, the business you are really in.

It's not the "dental" business. Dentistry is the deliverable. It's the "service" you or your associates and employees provide. Besides, dentistry is not a business. It's a sub-industry of healthcare. It could also be considered part of the "wellness" industry. Since, much of what dentists can do for their patients is helping them achieve wellness by repairing problems. The wellness approach is like playing offense. If all you ever do is make repairs, you're playing defense.

According to research and IBISworld.com, Dentistry is a $125-billion industry. There's so much money in dentistry, that it's attracting a lot of attention - more than ever before –from business-minded folks. The big money on Wall Street and investors worldwide are starting to pay more attention.

In my report released in September of 2013, *The State of Dentistry*, which is now the preface to this book, I went into specific details about why dentistry is, again, becoming a target of change advocates.

Dentistry was once a "cottage" industry that solo dentists dominated. Today, the shift from solo and group practices to chain-owned offices is becoming ever more apparent, and the industry has allowed it to happen. It's no longer a matter of "when," but how fast.

I witnessed the change early. I could see the movement from solo practice where a dentist could earn a nice $150,000 to $250,000 or more per year and live a life on their terms to now, where new graduates are saddled with huge debts, have zero business experience *and* the expectation that they have a "right" to a $200,000+ a year income.

That's a great dream, but it's far from reality. The cost to open a small three-op office, in basic equipment alone, sets a dentist or businessman like me back

$120,000 or more. That doesn't include any advanced diagnostic equipment – just the basics. Then, layer on tenant improvements, a monthly lease payment, staffing costs (you can't work by yourself – but I do have one Member that does *and* pulls it off; she's incredible and highly unusual), insurances, and all the supplies required, and you're looking at $500,000 in the blink of an eye. Maybe more, depending on location.

Of course, you also need reserves. They'll keep you afloat during the first 6 months of operation.

Unless you're already wealthy coming out of dental school, you'll be challenged to make this work.

It's not impossible. But, it's a tall order. Especially if your advanced education consists of 3.9 years of clinical instruction and 0.1 years of actual business instruction taught by folks who are unlikely to be *real* entrepreneurs and who, in all likelihood, have never actually started and/or operated a profitable practice.

Experienced dentists, too, are facing a tough market to find star employees (this is, without question, the #1 challenge in ANY business, and so it goes for dentistry), new patients who keep their appointments, unreasonable insurance reimbursements and, for far too many, a built-in unwillingness to WANT to be "in business" and not "in practice." As author, Jack Stack, (*The Great Game of Business*) says, "You gotta wanna." And, for those who don't *wanna* be in business, the income disparity is enormous.

Some Members of my Clear Path Society® have $3/4-

million or more in take-home pay and they no longer practice. Others struggle to earn $100,000 a year being a dentist in their own office. Those at the top of the income pyramid are entrepreneurs first, and dentists second, if at all. The others are still figuring it out. They usually do. Acceptance and understanding of this do not come easy for a person that wants to be a clinician.

A key factor that shouldn't be lost on those in the upper echelons of my Membership: They all practice and create habits based on successful behaviors. They don't engage in self-defeating behaviors. They're not drunks or drug addicts. They have solid marriages (not one is divorced and not one has a spouse in their office unless they are a fellow dentist). They're spiritual. Most attend church. They are practiced leaders who are engaged in ongoing leadership development and who set high expectations of those around them. They don't tolerate mediocrity. They measure everything and establish baselines to improve upon. They are comfortable around and with the idea of having a lot of money. They are ambassadors for and proud to participate in supporting the very communities they practice in.

YOU have a choice. You can be the technician or you can be the entrepreneur. No matter how great of a clinician you are, there's an income limit. There is NO income limit on being an entrepreneur. That all boils down to your ambition and implementation.

This book is for the dentist entrepreneur (or the one in training.)It'll lay down a number of foundation principles you can quickly adapt to your needs. You'll find honest, blunt truth telling. This book is based not on boardroom thoughts, overnight Internet sensations without any practical experience, or, ivory tower theories espoused by false experts, but instead based on reality. A successful, profitable, reality.

Before you finish the book, be sure to take advantage of the generous free offers my co-authors have been kind enough to include.

I'd also suggest, should one or all of them appeal to you, reach out to them. They're in this book because what they do works.

What is Marketing & Why it's Important

For the analytical readers of this book, I'll provide a textbook definition of marketing. Google says marketing is defined as, "the action or business of promoting and selling products or services, including market research and advertising."

To me, everything you do in your practice, with and for your team, your patients and your community, is marketing. Everything. Yes, marketing by my definition is broad. All actions you take to imprint your brand and your culture on the people in your community is marketing. Included in that is the type of staff you have – what they look like, act like, do in their spare time and more. It's all marketing.

Similar to my definition of marketing, my definition of "selling" might surprise you. In my experience, everyone associated with you is selling something all the time. They just don't know it and haven't had it framed properly to understand it that way.

Examples: You sell your staff on staying in their positions at your office. You do this unconsciously every day. You sell your patients on staying in your practice. You and your team sell patients on treatment they need or want and then you sell them on returning and referring. If you're like the vast majority of dentists and other businessmen, odds are, you do it poorly or can improve. I've yet to meet a businessman or woman that can't improve their selling skills or their marketing skills, so don't be insulted.

Poor marketing, poor selling skills and absence of leadership are the biggest reasons that cause many businesses to fail. This includes dental offices that close their doors in cities and towns where another dental office is thriving down the street.

You've no doubt heard the comparison story about two dentists in different towns. It bears repeating to make a point. So, here goes: One dentist is successful. He has a great staff and all the gadgets. His income is among the highest 1% of dentists nationwide.

A fellow graduate from dental school in another town has a miserable practice. His income is in the lowest 10%. He has terrible staff. His patients are terrible. They won't accept treatment and, to top it off, the economy is bad.

Take the failing dentist, stick him in the successful dentist's office and, in under a year, the failing dentist will take that successful practice down to nothing. The great staff will leave. The income will drop. Patients will leave. The local economy will begin to look like garbage.

Meanwhile, the successful dentist, in that same year, has turned around the failing office. He's replaced the staff, hired a great new team, he's selling a half-dozen implants a week, more Invisalign® cases are being started every day and the practice is hugely profitable.

I actually know several dentists that do what I just described for a living. They buy troubled offices, fix 'em and sell 'em. It's a great niche with nice paydays if you like moving around.

Get the drift? It's rarely the location. It's rarely the economy. It's rarely "the type of patients." It's usually the attitude and behaviors we engage in.

Chapter 2

Two Types of Marketing

There are two types of marketing in my world: internal and external.

Internal marketing is directed at existing patients or those people who are inside the walls of your practice to keep them engaged with you (retention of existing patients.)Examples: Internal signage, patient events, a patient newsletter (if you're not doing a patient newsletter, I can guarantee you're leaving big money on the table and amassing a huge number of neglected relationships), or a weekly email to existing patients. It's what you must do to link patients to you, forever. In-office financing you offer can be considered marketing if it's done right.

External marketing are efforts directed at anyone, via *advertisements,* who is not a patient, to entice, induce or outright gift/bribe them to try your office out (I call that removing "barriers.") Examples include print advertising, websites, direct mail, Internet search directories, AdWords by Google, Bing advertising and more. These efforts are designed to raise awareness, create curiosity and evoke feelings of, "I want/need that."

I'll dive more into the top internal and external marketing tactics later in this book, and, several of my co-authors will explore their areas of expertise in patient attraction and retention, and how they integrate into today's successful, profitable practice.

Meanwhile, I have a number of rules every external ad must adhere to.

Primarily, an ad must create traceable revenue. If it cannot provide a traceable ROI (return-on-investment), I won't do it. Period. No ifs ands or buts.

(Later in this book, I'll actually reveal my entire checklist I use to evaluate every ad I create, review or place for my own office or that of my Members or soon, Franchisees.)

Therefore, if marketing is defined as all actions you take to imprint your brand and your culture on the people in your community, then what is 'advertising?'

Advertising is the engagement of defined intentional efforts – ads, etc. – made by you and your team to increase the brand awareness of your practice, your business and by inducing new patients to take action, be it calling you, emailing you, etc., to demand an appointment.

NOTE: Existing patients should also be presented with regular advertisements (whether you are promoting a free report about a specific topic or directly asking them to take action and invest in optional services) to keep them coming back and engaging with your business. In my office, we have a monthly newsletter that is mailed to every active patient and a monthly offer that goes out by mail (we use full-color, large postcards), too.

Chapter 3

How to Stand Out & Capture More of Your Market

One of the oldest tricks in the book – it goes back hundreds of years – to create differentiation and capture a unique piece of any market is to build your own celebrity brand.

There are a number of ways to do this. Write a book. Speak. Volunteer. Work with high-profile patients (and not keep it a secret).

One of my advisors told me a simple way to accomplish this was to be somewhere and be somebody.

The highest income earners in every field are paid for WHOM they are. It has zero to do with clinical skills. In fact, I can be the highest compensated dental office owner in America and not be a dentist. In America, I have the opportunity to earn more than any dentist does and I never have to spend a day in dental school. I can be paid for WHO I am and who I've built myself up to be – through experience, unique promotions and more.

This same strategy can work for you on a local level. It works very well for my clients who embrace this idea – that people will seek you out for WHO you are not WHAT you are. That's a tough pill to swallow. But, it's reality.

One of my Members has used his mission trips to faraway lands as a major lever to capture the attention of his local TV and radio stations. As they've gotten to know him, they've come to love him. They love his staff. He is now their expert dentist. He is loved for the WHO, not the WHAT.

Are his clinical skills better than any other dentist in his community? Maybe. Maybe not. Frankly, his existing patients and those new patients he attracts couldn't care less. They are going to him because... "He's the GUY." They want to be associated with him. They want to have bragging rights to their friends and family.

Other examples you might be familiar with to help me

drive home this point:

The Wizard of Oz...

Are Drs. Roizen and Oz the best physicians in the world? No. Someone out there is better, smarter, but they are very likely making a fraction of what either of these two marketing geniuses does.

Why?

Patients seek them out for WHO they are, not their expertise. Their expertise is assumed. They are, famous. They are celebrities. They are paid for WHO, not what.

The Kardashians, love 'em or hate 'em, are not paid for any sort of expertise at all. They are a multi-million dollar enterprise for WHO they are. Not what they are. In fact, they have no discernable expertise.

Like it or not, that's the culture we're in. A celebrity culture and, if you're clever, motivated and desire to be at the top of your game, you'll embrace this and exploit it. You won't fight it.

Chapter 4

The Most Important Position in Your Dental Office

If you had to wager a guess, who would you think is the single most important person in your office aside from the patient, on a daily basis?

You, the doctor?

Your DA?

Your hygienist?

Who?

From a tough, long, ugly experience, I can, without hesitation, tell you the single most important person in your dental office is who most refer to as the Office Manager. The COO (Chief Operations Officer) of the practice.

In my world, you have an office manager or you have a practice that you're setting up for failure.

In other words, having a competent, honest, hard-working, reliable, all-knowing office manager is the KEY to your future financial success.

If you believe your office is too small to have one, I'd argue all day long that you're wrong, especially if you're the technician (clinical dentist) in your practice and not just the owner. Heck, even if you're like me and are just the owner of the dental office, if you don't have an office manager, you're setting yourself up for burnout and failure. Plain and simple.

I can point to numerous clients of mine, many of whom do multiple six figures each month, with a number of them closing in on SEVEN figures a month, and they all, every single one of them, have a dedicated office manager. In a couple of cases, they have more than one. I can also point to GPs doing $50,000 a month with office managers. And guess what? Their office is growing, AND, it's profitable. AND, the doctor has no cause or reason to burn out. Why? He's focused on clinical. He delegates everything else (except the checkbook – never delegate the check-writing responsibilities!).

I'm at my dental office for no more than two to three times a week and I'm rarely there for more than ten to fifteen minutes at a time. Some weeks, I don't even go in. (I took a ten day vacation recently and that month ended up being our best, most profitable month ever and I wasn't even there!)

Yet, I have my finger on the pulse of the office – from new patient numbers, production, collections, and more. I get a report every day. I look at the P&L and Balance Sheets every single day. It takes me no more than fifteen minutes to review my numbers. That's it. Every aspect of that is systemized and provided to me by the COO.

Here's a key point: It's not just reviewing the numbers. It's understanding how to *influence* and move the numbers in the direction they need to go.

If it were up to me to do what my COO does, I'd struggle as I did for way too long with mediocrity.

A quick story: I promoted a crackerjack chairside DA to become the office manager. My partner and I worked with her for two years on trying to develop her into a leader and a manager. It just didn't take. We'd put her in a position where she couldn't win and we didn't take action quick enough to end it. She was the right person in the wrong job.

Finally, we were backed into a corner. Both of us had had enough. Two days before I left the state to conduct a three-day seminar for my Members and clients, we fired her. Only two days before that, we'd found our answer via a killer craigslist ad, and, we attracted exactly the right person we were looking for.

Fast forward nearly 8 months later and the business has completely transformed into what I always wanted but could never quite get my former office manager to see. Helene has done an incredible job. I can't say enough about her and the way she has conducted herself.

I even know, personally, office managers that have had zero dental experience step in and become successful. They come from retail environments, other medical environments, bus dispatch barns (one of the best office managers I've ever met) and more.

Your perfect office manager might come from another dental office. Then again, they might come from Nordstrom's.

Just remember: like any position in your office you must have filled, you can teach *skills*, but you can't teach attitude, determination, honesty, integrity and guts. Just make sure whomever you hire has what you can't teach. Then, set them up for success, not failure. Don't be greedy – share the wealth. Give them authority and show them you trust them to do their job.

No matter what though, you can trust, but ALWAYS verify. Your office manager can make or break your practice. They can turn a terrible business around (given time and support). They can also ruin a great business. I have a simple motto when it comes to hiring: *Hire Fast. Fire Fast.* It's living by what my friend Lee Milteer calls, "A swift sword."

Chapter 5

A Checklist for Successful Ads

B elow is a partial list of requirements, elements and considerations, with my notes, we require of nearly every direct mail ad before they are deployed for my Wellness Springs Dental® offices or for my Private Clients and Members(This goes for most other ads as well. NOTE: not all aspects of this list are applicable to every ad.):

✓ Color or B/W? Test it. Paper Texture? Test it. Colored Paper/Stock? Test it. Know audience.
  o Color ads are what the majority do. To stand out and create a *pattern interrupt*, consider sparse color with a focus on black ink and an unusual design (a Retro look, for example).

✓ Direct Mail Postage: Live Stamp or Metered?
  o Test. Live stamps usually outperform metered postage for "A-pile" mail. A-pile mail is mail that generally replicates mailings from a friend instead of mass mailings. Hand-written address with hand-applied/crooked commemorative stamp preferred vs. inkjet or laser addressed (not preferred, but often unavoidable).

✓ Direct inkjet onto mailing piece, use a label or hand-address? Test. When possible, use hand-addressed to improve open rates of letter mail and read rates of postcards.

✓ Testimonials
  o Every ad, where space permits, should have relevant testimonials. Use, when possible, real full name and city/state.

✓ White Space – Use all available real estate
  o At my company, Jerry Jones Direct, our designs mimic classic direct response advertising, where all available white space is used to tell the story and move the reader to action. *White space does not sell.* Relevant words, illustrations and photos sell. Beware of those who insist on large amounts of white space.

✓ Benefit-driven copy
  o Feature-laden copy is most often used in ads designed by big corporate ad agencies and most who have no experience in truly understanding what moves prospects to

action. This type of copy merely describes the features of a product or service and not what it will DO for the prospective client – the *benefits* of its use or application. No picture is painted about how life might be easier, etc. Leaving that to the imagination of your prospect is dangerous and ineffective.

✓ Visible, easy-to-understand offer
  o Too often, we expect too much of a single ad. The primary purpose of any ad is to get the reader to take action. Use caution with what action you ask of your reader and the number of options you give them in the way of an offer (and how they should respond to your offer). Your offer should be clear and simple. It should also be an attractive, exciting and interesting offer that reverses the risk to the reader (in other words, you, as the business owner, should shoulder the risk of the patient trying your office out).

✓ One offer or Multiple?
  o If multiple, are they separated by Coupon Borders? Try to keep focus on just ONE if possible. Be sure it's a CLEAR, easy-to-understand offer. It's rare a two- or three-offer ad will out pull a single-focused ad that concentrates the reader's attention on a single choice. More choices can lead to inaction on the part of your prospect.

✓ Photos of patients (ACTUAL patients only)
  o Use real photos. Stock photos should be a last resort. Be sure to add a caption to every

photo even if it's simply describing the who and what. Readers' eyes are naturally drawn to captions, making them one of the most read parts of any ad.

✓ Does Headline stand on its own and is it compelling enough to get the prospect's butt off the couch?
- o Headlines are the single most important part of any ad.
- o A headline appears at the top of the ad and is used as a calling card to draw interested prospects to the ad.
- o A poor or missing headline generally renders any ad useless.
- o A practice name or doctor's name is not an ad headline.
- o Front and back of postcard can offer different headlines, but they still need to be powerful

✓ Tracking Phone Numbers: Vanity and/or local number (Front and Back)
- o Every ad should have a unique, local (when appropriate) tracking phone number. You should use a service like MessageMetric.com that allows you to add an unlimited number of tracking numbers among other amazing features like call recording (so you can coach your team) and more. Not using tracking numbers compromises the real stats an ad may produce.

✓ Return Address: (Use MAP, too)
- o Include your business address. On direct mail to prospective patients, be sure to

include a simple, easy-to-read map that shows your office's location relative to other local, popular landmarks.

✓ Does it contain Unknowns? i.e. CEREC Crowns, other technical words, etc.

    o Dentists and other technical professionals with their own "language" are known to include what I call product or service unknowns in ads. DO NOT. Use layman's terms and always write your ad copy at a level a 6th grader can understand. This allows prospects to skim and get the point of your ad. And, no, your patients are not more sophisticated than this when it comes to ads. I sell to dentists just like you and I've never written an ad at any higher level of reading comprehension than the 6th grade. Communicating at this level helps avoid confusion.

✓ Offer Deadline. Limited Availability.

    o Repeat offer on front and back of ad to ensure immediate response. Stay within fifteen days if mailing a local offer or driving traffic to websites using deadlines. The longer your deadline is from the drop date, the less important it will appear to your prospect. You want them to act now, not later. Help them prioritize calling you by having a tight deadline. In addition, it helps if your offer has limited availability. Example, "This offer is valid for only the first nineteen new patients that call." Be sure to include a reason "why" only nineteen can be accepted, and always accept more than nineteen if you have the chance! Never turn away a new patient!

✓ Use of starburst for offer to make it stand out
  o This important, often-neglected, design element helps browsers get pulled into the full context of the ad.

✓ Value of offer (Regular price, etc.)
  o State the real value of the offer if someone were to walk into your office off the street. This builds value and, in many states, it's a required part of any ad for dental services, as is stating the dentist making the offer is a general dentist or not. Be sure you are familiar with and understand your state's requirements for dental advertising.

✓ Ensure main offer is under $100
  o To maintain a low barrier of entry, it's best to keep initial new patient offers under the $100 threshold. Free offers often still work best. Test all price points. If using a free exam offer, be sure relevant copy is included in the ad to help reader understand that any "fixes" or treatment that is found will need to be paid for. We use some well-written, highly effective copy to achieve this on our free exam offers and it helps prepare them to pay for their treatment.

✓ Source Coding.
  o Be sure to include a source code in your ad, so your staff will know what ad has

generated the call. For example, "Mention or BRING this postcard with you at your appointment and receive..." or mention "April Showers" when you call. Tracking numbers also help to determine which ads are most effective.

✓ If mailing a postcard, does the card state: "Please Turn Over" on the address side?

✓ Does "Offer valid for new patients only" appear on the card in all applicable places?
   o Offer-limiting copy. Use sparingly, keep fine print to a minimum. Be sure to include an offer for existing patients – for example, $43 off next appointment, etc.

✓ Manage your expectations

   o Be careful what you're asking of your ads. A great ad can generate a large number of calls when it hits the right audience in the right media. It's your team's job to convert those calls to appointments and those appointments to paid treatment. My Clear Path Society® Members all have access to monthly staff and doctor phone coaching. In addition, each receives my $3,000 10-Point Phone Success Training, a 13-CD system with workbook and flip chart with LIVE lifetime phone coaching.

Chapter 6

The Best, Most Cost-Effective, Source for New Patients

There are a number of activities every business, whether dental office or not, should undertake to achieve maximum referrals from its patients or clients. In fact, most if not all of the internal marketing strategies mentioned in this book will work for any client- or patient-based business.

While what I'm about to cover in Internal Marketing is a great starting point for you, it's not an all-encompassing, exhaustive list. You'll very likely have more to add of your own! And, you should be exploring and experimenting with additional methods to add to this list.

Internal Marketing

Newsletter, Postcards/Direct Mail. Most offices do some sort of newsletter. The problem is that most do it poorly, often resulting in the doctor believing his efforts are ineffective or that the idea of sending a newsletter is ineffective. There's a reason why newsletters are at the top of my internal marketing list. They work when done properly. In my office, we also send a monthly offer, using a postcard, to our existing patients in addition to our monthly newsletter.

Signage. Often not given enough credit, point of sale signage or signs at different counters and inside operatories can be effective at increasing referrals or other desired outcomes. Some of these might include monthly specials, invites to seminars or other important information about your practice patients should know. Restaurants use table tents very effectively to highlight their profitable offerings. When done right, this can help introduce new products or services to your existing patients, which should increase referrals or additional income from added treatment. Signage is best when rotated out every four to six months so patients are seeing something new at each visit.

Buttons. Remember the buttons that some folks wore?(Want a whiter smile? Ask me how!) These can help introduce new products and begin conversations that can be converted into sales. Buttons worn on scrubs can be a simple, effective way for your staff and patients to engage in a conversation about whitening, sedation, sleep apnea, snoring treatments and more. Seems corny? It's only corny until you close your first $5,000 sleep apnea case or start moving two to three or more $199+ whitening treatments a day. Soon, you'll have buttons for every service you offer.

Conversation/Suggestion. While this is a no-brainer, it's amazing how few doctors and staff use a simple conversation to lead to something far better for themselves and their patients. One of the easiest things in the world to do is read a new patient intake form that details a patient's chief concerns. Then, begin a conversation by saying, "You indicated on your form you'd like a whiter smile. Have you ever considered a simple whitening treatment?" That alone can open the door to chairside or, at the very least, take-home whitening. A recent evaluation in my dental office revealed that every take-home whitening we do is worth $150 to the office in profit. That's on the low-end and doesn't take into consideration chairside whitening profits!

Excitement. If you and your team are not excited about what you do and the results you achieve for your patients, they won't be either. You must convey enthusiasm and excitement constantly and continuously. If you're having a crappy day, fake it until you make it. Patients can read you and smell tension a mile away. They'll no more say "yes" to

ANY treatment plan you propose if your head's not in the game than they would voluntarily undergo a colonoscopy. If your numbers are down, look at yourself first, then your team. If one of you is not in the game, get in it or get benched. No patient will refer another friend or family member to a toxic environment. Fix this and your referrals will increase. Almost immediately.

Events. One of my co-authors, Dr. Darold Opp, has created an ingenious way to involve an entire community in a referral movement. I'll let Darold explain that in his chapter. I can tell you from experience I have done what Darold does on a small scale and it was incredible for us. In fact, we've done it more than once and both times, it was a huge success. Learn more about it in Darold's chapter.

Reactivation. Every dentist in America with a practice older than twelve months is sitting on a goldmine of undone treatment. I've conducted a hundred or more undone treatment campaigns for my clients and Members and they are almost ALWAYS big winners that provide a major cash flow surge. Consider this: Any patient who does not have a next appointment is inactive and must be attended to. We'll go to extraordinary lengths and invest hundreds, even thousands of dollars to get patients back that know, like and trust us. For my own office and the vast majority of my Members, it's always a huge ROI. If it does not work for you, that's telling of a bigger problem that you must identify before you can move to the next level or profitability. My Clear Path Society® Members have access to my proven patient reactivation system as part of their benefits. It includes a number of direct mail pieces as well as a telephone script. The direct mail copy can also be converted over to emails, so that you address patients via an electronic method and good old-fashioned mail. Now, that said, don't get cheap and expect email to have anywhere near the impact a direct mail piece will... Both together are always better. Moreover, if I had to choose one, I'd choose direct mail.

Referral contests. One of fastest ways to get your patients talking about you is to create a horse race scenario —you know, a referral contest with a prize that is reasonable enough to get folks interested and excited. We've done these in the past and given away free TVs, bicycles, iPads, gift certificates and the like. There are dozens of ways to run the contests and I don't think there is a "bad" way to do one. Just make sure you promote it in the office, your team talks about it, and both referred and referring patients are recognized and rewarded for their participation. Keep your state dental board policies in mind and don't break the rules.

Recognition. One of the coolest ways to get people more interested in what you're doing is to show recognition to others in your practice. That means employees and patients alike. It also means recognizing others in your community that do great things. You can do this in your newsletter every month (and should be) as well as in press releases to local media and on a special wall in your office. There's nothing quite like seeing your name in lights and, when patients or your staff see theirs, it has a huge impact that they feel compelled to share with others.

Video/Documentary. Another great technique for internal marketing is to highlight who and what you are and, more importantly, what others think of you in a video documentary. I don't want to steal my co-author, Ron Sheetz's thunder, so I will let him explain in detail how a video documentary of your practice can be the ultimate differentiator between you and every other dentist in the world.

Referrals from other sources (Chiropractors, MDs, etc.). The opportunity to create a referral network with other patient-based professionals in your community is not taken advantage of nearly enough. Not a phony network, but a real, valuable, educated network of professionals that know what you do, why and how and whom specifically you can help. There's no better way to do this that good ol' gumshoe marketing. Pounding the pavement, having lunches and setting up friendships and partnerships that are mutually beneficial. MOST professionals feel alone and by themselves, so when you reach out and offer to refer to them, and DO refer to them, often, a strong individual will do the same in return. Particularly if you educate them about the advances in dentistry and the problems you solve for your patients. It's not a one and done deal. This network is something you'll need to invest time and effort into. But, why not?

Social Media. While I'm not a fan of Facebook, Twitter or any other internet-based social media platform, I do have Members that occasionally make it pay. While it's "free," don't confuse it as not having a cost to you. It does. If you have a staff member that manages it, there's time involved (wages) and lost opportunity (what else could that person be doing that could be more effective at generating revenue?). If YOU are managing it, that's even worse. As a dentist, you should be busting out treatment and doing what no one else in your office can do. Gaining "likes" and such on Facebook, Twitter and other social media sites is a huge waste of time and money. Especially so, considering you should be producing $500 or more per hour. Also, be wary of the advice you hear about how to use it. Most advice is flawed and is typically promulgated by people who have zero practical experience in direct response marketing.

Don't buy into investing your valuable time in attracting "likes" to your Facebook page. Instead, if you're determined to use Facebook, use it for its ability to target the avatar patient you want in ads they offer. You can learn more about that from my co-author and Internet wunderkind, Matt Prados. To me, this is the only real value of Facebook.

Chapter 7

Going Outside: External Marketing to Attract New Patients

Once you have implemented a number of internal marketing strategies to attract patients referred by your existing patients, you can move on to external marketing. However, I'd caution you to exploit fully every internal marketing opportunity before moving on for two reasons: internal marketing generally requires less capital and it routinely yields a more motivated patient due to the transfer of relationship that occurs when an existing patient refers a friend, family member or colleague to you.

External Marketing

Direct Mail. A question I hear from dentists more often than any other about direct mail is: Isn't it expensive?

The second most common thing I hear from dentists about direct mail is that it doesn't work in their area. It might shock you when I say, both are 100% right. What you believe about it is true for you until you're proven wrong. I can tell you that direct mail has built more dental practices from scratch and grown mature dental practices larger than any other external marketing method available save for, perhaps, insurance companies. In my twenty years in the dental industry, I've mailed millions of pieces of direct mail for my own office and for my Members, generating over a hundred of thousand patients. It continues, to this day, in the midst of the Internet explosion, to be an incredibly reliable method of new patient attraction in nearly every market in America.

If it's not working for you, there's a reason why and, it can only be because of one of three reasons: the message you're sending doesn't resonate with the person receiving it (wrong prospect); you're sending it in the wrong format; or, you're sending it to the place. Is direct mail expensive? Yes, it is very expensive when it does not work, but when it does, it delivers the highest quality external marketing patients possible. There are a number of reasons why that is, not the least of which is that folks who respond to direct mail are readers. They are educated. They have a need you've identified and they are hot and ready to go. In other words, when your direct mail works, it's an incredibly effective and economical new patient magnet!

Here are a few examples of other external marketing sources my Clear Path Society Members and I regularly rely on for new patients:

Newspapers/Print Media (magazines and newspapers). Like yellow pages, far too many have drank the Kool-Aid® and believe newspaper ads and even print media in general are dead. Like yellow page ads, the response rates from print media, predominately newspapers, is in fact, declining. Readership is declining. I am sure most newspapers would prefer to shutter their printing plants, but the fact remains that in the vast majority of markets, newspapers and other print media remain viable sources from which to generate new patients.

Case in point, my own city's newspaper. Every month, without fail, we're in it. At the very least, a free standing insert. Some months, full-page ads. There are still 40,000+ subscribers and papers printed every day. Of those 40,000, I only need ONE to accept treatment based on our advertising rates. It's almost unfair, isn't it?

When the economics line up like this, I'm all for testing and running ads in every media you can find...even the ones most proclaim to be dead. That's the great thing about dentistry – you don't need ten, fifteen or one-hundred and fifty new patients from an advertising source to make it worthwhile. I encourage you to approach every media with this thought: If I can get a patient from it, one that will be around for years, pay their bill and refer others, really, how many do I need?

In newspapers, I'll typically test a general new patient ad first. If we have success with that, then I'll niche market in the publication next time. In other words, I'll promote a specific benefit gained from a procedure like dentures, implants or orthodontics.

I'd suggest the same plan of attack with every new media you test: general ad first, then niche it. Some media you'll find only work with one or the other. Other media will work with both. Demographics, size of readership and reach will be among the determining factors.

Yellow Pages. If you're in a big city, say, over 250,000 people, this strategy may not apply. However, if you're like me, you'll want to test it to prove it wrong. In fact, every ad media you can find, you should at least test it to see if it's a potentially valuable source for you or not.

I advise all of my Members, even if they've been out of it for years, to try to test a small 1/8, ¼, ½ or even a full-page ad in their yellow pages. And, test all of them. In some cities, that means you might be in three or four publications. Maybe more.

Our approach is to place a simple ad like this, to test results. We use a tracking number and we carefully listen to and review the calls regularly to make sure our $50/month investment is pulling before we place a larger ad:

Web (+ email follow-up). I suspended my Luddite beliefs a few years back and decided I'd finally make the interwebs a successful media for my dental office. To do that, I merely took what works for us in attracting new patients in offline media and put it online. Yes, it was that simple. Then, I found the #1 interwebs and online marketing expert, Matt Prados. Matt's been working magic in the healthcare niche online for years. I'll let him explain more about his online voodoo in his chapter. Then, without hesitation, I'd encourage you to contact him.

Radio. If there is one media that outweighs all but television, it's radio. It has the widest reach to a wide variety of audiences, all niched, based on station content/play. If you can get radio to work for promoting your dental practice, you have a virtually unlimited opportunity to run ads.

This holds true if you have more than one office (what I refer to as an ML/MD or multilocation/multi-doctor practice). I've asked my friend and leading radio-advertising expert, Fred Catona, to give you some tips on radio advertising in his chapter. It's one of the media my franchise will be focusing on as we build up locations in different metro areas to increase new patient flow and build our brand via direct response marketing.

Gum Shoe Marketing. A lost art, there's much to be said for distributing flyers in given areas or even door hangers. I have a client in the busy metropolis of Dallas, Texas, and he's had great success using a local service to place door hangers. It's been very economical and a useful media to get his new practice off the ground. A quick search on Google will reveal a number of national companies that offer flyer circulation and door hanger distribution. Don't knock it until you, yes, test it.

Press. One of my Gold Clear Path Society® Members, Dr. Sean Tarpenning, of Eau Claire, WI, has been very successful generating press for his dental office. He's experienced TV interviews, full-page articles on the front page of his local paper and more. If you were to ask him, he'd tell you there's no price he could put on all the free press he's been able to garner – but I'm sure it's easily in the tens of thousands and rapidly approaching the a hundred thousand in free press.

It really started when he offered to do Invisalign® for a local radio personality. From there, that leverage point blossomed into becoming the "go-to-dentist" for ALL local media, TV included, to interview their friend, "Dr. T.," when a dental health-related issue hits the media. It's a great gig and it started simply enough.

Press can be worked from this angle or from any number of other ways. One of my favorite methods for my own office is to issue press releases to all local media when we're going to do free dentistry days, our annual patient BBQ and Kids' Day or when a controversy hits the media. In that case, we're quick to issue an opinion and to be mentioned in any stories. If you watch for opportunities like this, you too can take advantage of the free press.

I'll turn you on to another national source called HARO, or helpareporterout.com. This website provides a number of opportunities for you to interface with local and national reporters.

Book Authorship. The ultimate positioning piece in any industry or market is becoming and being a published author, and the more books you have out, the better. Check out Nina Hershberger's chapter in this book about how to become an author.

Seminars/Speaking. Most dentists are completely unaware of the opportunity speaking provides. A number of my own Members hold regular implant and orthodontics or sleep apnea and snoring seminars in their offices.

My friend and Silver Clear Path Society Member, Dr. Scott Westermeier, is the go-to guy for this method of marketing. Scott's done well using seminars to create a large implant-based general practice. To learn more about Scott, drop an email

toseminars@jerryjonesdirect.com and in the
Subject Line, use: Implant Seminars.

Other People's Lists (OPL). An easy way to reach
a targeted, potentially health-conscious market,
who may not even know you exist, is to arrange for
endorsed mailings with other professionals in your
area that have client or patient lists.

This is easily done with chiropractors, plastic
surgeons, CPAs, attorneys and more. It's limited
only to your own imagination.

Endorsed mailings are most effective when one
professional sends a letter or note to their client list
about you. In turn, you do the same for them. The
idea is simply to create business for each other
using direct mail.

An important point to consider when doing
endorsed mailings is to be sure that you understand
that both the professional and potential new patient
will need to grasp the concept of WIIFM, or, what's
in it for me. Both parties need to have a clear and
acceptable "reason why" they should act and do
business with you.

Management of Marketing

Inter-Vergence Marketing. I can promise you
that no matter what book you might read about
dental marketing, none will address this concept of
marketing that you must understand and utilize to
make every dollar invested in marketing do the
work of two or more dollars.

Sounds crazy, right? I mean, how do you get leverage like that in marketing? Simple...

It's based on the concept I call "Inter-Vergence Marketing." What it means is undertaking marketing with similar messages in a number of different media at the same time, thereby getting what some might refer to as "convergence." However, when the promotions are similar and play off each other, they interrelate. Thus, the term, "Inter-Vergence."

Here's a quick example of how Inter-Vergence marketing plays out. We'll drop thousands of direct mail pieces and, in the same week, we'll drop freestanding inserts, release a radio ad campaign, initiate press releases designed to "hit" at the same time and release an aggressive online marketing campaign where we are on every website a resident in a target area is on. In addition, we'll layer on email marketing, too.

The message sent is similar. The brand is everywhere and, our messages hit with a blinding punch. *The result?* A huge surge of new patients. A campaign like this might run $15,000 or more. It's also designed to kick off a sustained, long-term campaign of direct mail, newspaper ads, FSIs, etc., just like those that we use at my own Wellness Springs Dental® of Salem office.

Note: This advanced marketing strategy that should not be deployed without professional guidance and a strategic focus on the content and timing of the messages.

Infusionsoft. Managing any marketing campaign and keeping it running on time, in-sync and measurable, using what was once a hated application (by me) is today, required. At Jerry Jones Direct, if you've read an email from me or received direct mail, Infusionsoft (IS) managed the process.

In my mind, IS stands alone in the world of CRM (customer relationship management software). Not only can it text, call, email or assign tasks, what it really does is liberate you from day-to-day drudgery and system failures in your marketing and in your business. I'll defer to my friend, co-author and expert IS guy, Loren Smith. *To learn more about IS, email IS@JerryJonesDirect.com.*

People. It seems basic that without incredible people in your practice, it will fail. At best, it will limp along sucking the life out of you (and emptying your wallet). How do I know this? I have very intimate, first-hand, knowledge.

Quick story to make my point: I suffered for years with one business thinking it'd survive and thrive if only I threw more money at it. It did – it thrived taking my money. And there was no one to blame but me. I thought management was more competent than it was. They thought I had pockets that I didn't mind digging into. We were both wrong. In a final effort to save the business, I fired the manager and hired a *real* operations officer, all in one week. A few months later, the problems were largely all cleared up: the new Chief Operations Officer hired new staff members and we had a P&L

and Balance Sheet that ought to be the envy of every business owner around.

I made the right hire, gave her authority to make changes and got the heck out of her way. It's that simple in concept. (But simple doesn't mean easy, right?)

Great people can make you look like a superstar. The wrong person in the wrong job can make you appear a fool. In fact, if you suffer those fools long, like I did, you will be the fool.

This leads me to: Hire great people. Don't tolerate mediocrity.

I'll go one step further in managing your marketing. Make sure you have your staff/team filled in on what's going out, when, where and to whom. Include your COO and your newest and least paid team members, too. Your people can also help make a losing campaign a winner (by asking for, and getting, referrals). The wrong people can turn a winning marketing campaign into a loser. I've seen it and it's not pretty.

Results/Is it paying? The only thing that really matters when measuring the results of your marketing is this: IS THERE AN ROI? Is your marketing making money? All other considerations, like brand building, are second, third, or, irrelevant. I'll save congruence from this list as I believe your marketing must be congruent. It should look similar. Use your logo at every opportunity, but it never should it be the major focus and rely on a

USP (Unique Selling Proposition) you've developed for your business. What makes YOU unique relative to the thousands of other dentists out there).

I judge an ad to pay for itself and merit another run if the revenue produced is, at a minimal level, $2 of income for every $1 in expense (ad creation and placement cost) or 2:1.

I hear it repeatedly from Members: One of the great things about Clear Path Society® is that Members get pre-tested ads to run. Much of the risk is diluted. Anytime you can find a deal like that, where someone else has invested their own money to create and test an ad, and it worked for them, give it a shot yourself. You're far better off starting from a known than creating from scratch and investing in an unknown ad.

Who/expertise. During your journey to grow your practice, you'll come across partners and experts who will be with you forever.

Regardless of whom you engage to help you promote you practice, you need to hold them accountable for doing what they say they will do. In other words, hold their feet to the fire. Keep vendors/partners, your team, your spouse, your kids and your patients accountable. Don't tolerate anything less.

Be compassionate, but understand that your banker and your retirement account couldn't care less about the "why" behind such small bank deposits, which are a result of not holding yourself and those around you 100% accountable.

While I've invited the co-authors of this book to share their expertise with you, whomever you ultimately hire or collaborate with to reach the levels of success you desire, make sure they have real data and feedback from current or past clients that paints them in a positive light.

Always follow the advice of my college literature professor, Dr. David Boersma: "Make sure you always have your built-in, shock-proof shit detector on high alert."

Dental Insurance

Books could be written on the ins and outs of dental insurance. In fact, there are excellent newsletters published on the subject.

The reason I've included dental insurance in a book on dental success is that, in today's marketplace, survival without accepting assignment or working in some capacity with dental insurances is tenuous at best. Yes, it is possible to operate a profitable practice without accepting assignment or even engaging in a phone call with a dental insurance company. However, it's a rough road to travel and a very expensive one in most circumstances.

I've always recognized dental insurance for what it is: a media that costs you nothing to participate in, until you get a patient. Then, like any other media, you pay a fee. In this case, it's a discount. If you want their money and their patients, the insurance company will ask you to accept a discount off your UCR fees.

Some discounts are enormous. Others are reasonable for the transaction that has taken place.

My view: if you can operate a profitable practice accepting insurance (thus, a stream of new patients), why not? Why chase away something that pays if you hold up your end of the bargain?

Don't ignore the fact that my most successful Members and private clients accept assignment. They also have learned a thing or two about working with insurance companies to make it far more profitable, too.

In fact, I know more dentists that are successful *with* insurance than without. That tells you something.

For real leverage and generating more cash from insurance companies, I'll direct you to my client and friend's business, Dr. John Busby, of The Busby Consulting Group. John's MBA thesis focused on his interaction with insurance companies in his home territory of Madison, WI. Today, while John no longer needs to practice dentistry and, in fact, has relegated himself to management duties of his 8 doctor, two-location practice, he spends time working with dentists all over the US to improve their insurance company relationships. Be sure to read John's chapter in this book.

Chapter 8

Successful Management of a Dental Practice in a PPO Environment

By John Busby, D.D.S

One hires a financial advisor to invest retirement money or a physician to promote health and minimize illness. The same holds true for a dental practice. They hire advisors to help forecast future dental trends and participate in those trends successfully. Currently, the number one trend within the dental insurance world is PPO (preferred provider organization) penetration. Choosing to participate or not is critical to the financial success of every dental practice. It has been my experience that developing a strong relationship with dental insurance carriers will provide a thriving, prosperous source of patients and a positive influence on that dental practice's overall financial health.

It seems many dental providers choose to be in a state of denial about this trend. For many years, the mindset of dentists was that accepting a reduced fee for dental services was wrong and counterproductive. Any level of participation was an act against the best interest of dentistry as a whole. This is reinforced by the fact that many dentists manage small autonomous businesses and are very independent by nature. Like it or not, we are not immune to market forces. The choice to participate with PPO could be the most critical decision that a dentist will make. That decision needs to be based on knowledge and correct information rather that emotion. I'm Dr. John Busby and this the story of how that concept started for me, how it evolved and where the process stands today.

Delta Dental is the largest insurance carrier in Wisconsin and in many other states. The PPO business of Delta Dental of WI exceeds 60% of their total insurance coverage and 90% of all new dental insurance contracts. This trend is becoming undeniable and it is likely to increase as businesses are faced with decreasing monies for employee benefits. My theory is to embrace this form of dental insurance in order to diversify and stabilize the practice's patient base. By expanding the numbers of all patients (to include PPO patients) and expanding an enhanced fee schedule of

PPO plans, revenues are grown by increased patient numbers combined with increased insurance payments for all patients.

My dental group, Affiliated Dentists, S.C. (www.affiliateddentists.com) has employed associate doctors for many years. The challenge that every managing dentist has is to keep his or her associates busy. Younger associate dentists generally do not have the personal contacts to develop an active patient base without the managing dentist's help. We have had several associate dentists who have had open appointment times. I feel that the associate doctor and our group were at greater risk from having open appointments than from having reduced fees. In its simplest form, 85%+ of something is better than 100% of nothing. Fortunately, the dental world has strong operating margins. Even with an overhead of 55% of revenues, most industries would envy that level of residual margin, even with a reduced fee structure.

I felt so strongly about this idea, I participated in the ADA/Kellogg Business Management program from 2005-2006. This allowed me to engage the best business minds at Northwestern University's Kellogg Business School to challenge this theory. Affiliated Dentists essentially implemented this business model in 2004. As a result, I have over ten years of data to confirm overall success of this model. Any successful dental business model requires internal efficiency. This model will not be successful in a high overhead practice. A low overhead model allows flexibility to join PPOs and confirms that the overall business systems are intact, effective and functioning.

The number one question I receive is "why should I accept a reduced fee for a crown, a restoration or a prophylaxis?" To answer this question, one must have the mindset that we actually sell blocks of time in which we perform procedures rather than billing out a fixed dollar amount per procedure. Within those blocks of time, the key is to be more efficient and perform more procedures per unit of time. This is principle #1, which I will refer to as "Out Gun PPOs."

Another mistake is to think most PPO insurance companies will not pay a higher rate than the initial price offered. My ten-year track record shows consistent fee growth. Nearly every dental insurance company will negotiate a higher rate into becoming, what I will call, an enhanced fee. The enhanced fee schedule reflects principle #2, "Out Run PPOs."

Several observations I have made over the past ten years of dealing with dental PPO insurance companies:

Efficient practice management is critical. Overhead must be under control so residual margins are still profitable.

This practice model is helpful for multiple doctors in multiple locations. This allows for a larger capacity and flexibility. Insurance companies, historically, are more willing to work with groups than with solo practices.

It becomes more effective if a limited number of PPO providers participate in your area. There is no hard and fast rule on how many dentists per population is optimal for patient growth. Having no more than 10% of revenues from any one company is a guideline. If one company becomes so dominant in your practice that you cannot terminate, your leverage is greatly minimized.

The PPO does all of the marketing at no cost to your practice and directly sends patients to your practice, with a propensity to spend. If your practice has noted a limited number of new patients and limited revenue growth, that stagnation may be related to generalized attrition from PPO growth in your area.

If you provide outstanding care, PPO patients will refer friends, neighbors and colleagues. They frequently happily exceed their policy limits and demand non-covered procedures. If the patient changes employment, you are the standard to which future dental providers will be judged. Patients will return because of the quality of care and the personal connection that you provided. Did you provide a "Wow" factor? Do you have a unique marketing position? However dental care is packaged, it is one doctor taking care of one patient. The same is true of the interactions with all of your staff.

The larger your patient pool becomes the greater the leverage your practice has for future enhanced fee schedules. The insurance company will think "It is easier to keep us happy than attempt to replace us." A patient's greatest negotiation tool is the ability to walk away. In any negotiations, one must have an upside goal and a downside limit in mind before starting any level of discussions with an insurance company. Generally, that leverage occurs as a dental group acquires a greater volume of patients.

Adding PPO patients actually stabilize your practice by adding different pools and groups of patients. Vertical integration is segmentation by propensity to spend money and other socio-economic factors. Horizontal integration is the segmentation by employer groups. If one group experiences an economic downturn, that loss can be spread over multiple pools of people. This has the effect of minimizing risk and maintaining constant revenue and cash flow.

Affiliated Dentists is located in two suburbs of Madison, Wisconsin. We are primarily a fee-for-service practice. Our dentists generally do not know who the patient's insurance carrier is or if they have insurance at all. This is because our goal is to provide ideal dental care. That is based on patient needs, not the type of insurance, if any, that they hold. Dentists should never treat a patient differently based on insurance carrier or type. All dentists within a practice should treat all patients equally. Having only associate dentists treat PPO patients sends a poor subliminal message to doctors, staff and patients. If a patient is made to feel their treatment is substandard, all goodwill and all positives disappear.

The difference between the initial PPO fee and the growing "enhanced fee schedule" is all profit. I cannot emphasize this factor enough. An increase in fee structure immediately transfers to the bottom line. My goal is to expand the PPO fee schedule at twice the annual rate of inflation. Just as compounding interest and time is a plan for financial success, the same is true for PPO participation. Furthermore, I aim to be no more than 10% below the practice's UCR fees for most dental plans. I do not understand the logic of dentists who oppose PPO participation. Most practices already offer a 5% cash discount to patients and are willing to spend significant marketing dollars to acquire new patients, but will not accept a 10% reduced fee similar to a PPO fee.

Dentists have a tendency to be poor negotiators. They do not negotiate on a regular basis. In the office it is usually the "my way or the highway" approach. No insurance company will give a dental provider a significant increase in the first year; rather, they will make incremental increases over an extended time. This will achieve the same result. However, PPO participation needs to be thought of as a process rather than a one-year transition.

In my opinion, most dental fee structures are illogical. Many fees are set by comparing a fee for a procedure to other dental offices in the immediate area and/or zip code. Some dentists feel there is a more scientific approach. This involves purchasing a fee utilization service that places fees into a percentage of all fees submitted to insurance companies. The true determination of fees should be made based on complex analysis of materials used and time factor to produce the appropriate care. Presently there is little connection between a fee charged and the true effort and supplies used to accomplish the procedure.

Every dental insurance company has different formats for negotiation. Knowing what that format is and who the decision makers are creates efficiency. Insurance companies and their actuarial department have a unique language to communicate among themselves and dental providers. Knowing how to talk in insurance

"code" implies you know and respect the internal
working of that company.

The fee negotiator for the dental office must have the
ability to make an immediate decision on accepting or
requesting fees. Know your strategy prior to contacting
any insurance carrier. Be ready, willing and able to
make a decision if appropriate fees are offered.

Having a personal relationship with the insurance
company's negotiator is most helpful. I have visited the
offices of numerous insurance companies to meet with
their PPO fee negotiator. This may be impractical for
most, but I have chosen to differentiate our fee
negotiation group from all other negotiators. Other
dental consulting companies offer the same PPO fee
negotiation services as we do. However, I have a ten
year documented track record and business
relationships with the twenty-five largest PPO carriers
in my area. I guarantee no one can make the same
statement.

It is critical to change the mindset that PPOs are
negative. They are a different form of insurance
compensation. If your group is paid an appropriate fee
for dental care that is profitable, does the type of dental
insurance have any bearing at all? Adding PPOs to the
conventional fee-for-service mix adds stability and
provides the potential for growth.

The decision to participate in any insurance plan is a
complex issue. It has been my experience that an
aggressive PPO participation model can lead to
explosive growth, a consistent source of new patients
and stability to any dental practice. This is not for every

dental practice and not for most providers. It has been one of the best dental practice management decisions I have ever made on behalf of our dental group.

The Busby Consulting Group is a full-service dental consulting and business management firm for dental practices in a PPO environment. We are available to consult and provide direct fee negotiations to individuals and group practices.

The Busby Consulting Group's range of service includes:

- Initial Consultation –This will determine if PPO participation is right for you and your group, what number of carriers are appropriate to contact, and what realistic goals for our services might be.

- Full Service Fee Management–We will provide all levels of fee negotiation to increase PPO compensation to the maximum level and maintain those fees at the highest possible level for as many insurance companies as you desire. Our fee structure is based on the number of insurance carriers that you wish to negotiate with.

To learn more, contact The Busby Consulting Group:

> Dr. John Busby.
> Affiliated Dentists, S.C.
> 5601 Odana Road
> Madison, WI 53719
> BusbyConsultingGroup.com
> Work: 608-274-9077
> Cell: 608-217-4706
> JohnBusby7381@gmail.com

About The Author ...

John Busby- *has chosen to excel in the management of Dental Practices. After 36 years of managing dental organizations in the US Army and the private sector, Dr. Busby started the Busby Consulting Group. The consulting focus is on increasing the fee schedule of nearly every PPO for his clients. The chapter titled "Successful Management of a Dental Practice in a PPO Environment" is the shortened version of his M.B.A. thesis. As PPOs increase their dominance within the dental insurance world, having an expert to assist your dental practice is critical.*

Chapter 9

The 33 Trooths about Advertising for Dentists

By Fred Catona

The following are proven truths about advertising for new patients using radio:

1. Have a good vanity phone number, ideally one that spells a benefit and is 800 over any other prefix. Ex: 800 great smile. Avoid the words "to"

and "for" as they could be confused with two and four.

2. Your web address should be short and easy to remember.

3. Give yourself a unique moniker. Example: "Dr. Jerry White, your teeth's best friend."

4. If you have three or more office locations, use regular talk radio, sports and country radio formats to advertise on.

5. If you are small, use Pandora, Cable TV and direct mail.

6. An alternative, if you do not want to go it alone, is to chip in for advertising with other dentists and distribute the leads and profits.

7. Use a celebrity in your advertising or be a celebrity – set a world record for something, like I did!

8. Consider using a local, trusted celebrity.

9. Use a DJ as a special spokesperson (use him for your elephant offer – join us this June for our love-your-teeth cruise to the Bahamas.)

10. Know your enemies: cost, convenience and pain ...plus your competition and then market against them.

11. Advertise consistently. It is better to spend a little over a long period than a big splash and stop.

12. Advertising is accumulative; the more you do it, the more responses you'll get.

13. Advertising frequency equals trust and trust equals response.

14. Use a grabber in the first sentence of your commercial.

15. Ask two questions to pique interest in your commercial.

16. State your credibility in your commercial.

17. State your Unique Selling Proposition (USP) – your killer free offer.

18. Have three testimonials addressing your enemies in your commercial.

19. Use a controversial statement to wake up the listener.

20. Use an 800 phone number for your call to action.

21. Repeat your free offer.

22. Create urgency – "Limited-time offer."

23. Create scarcity to drive response immediately – "Free dental exam to the first fifty callers."

24. If you use music, only use it at the beginning of your commercial, not during your Call to Action (CTA).

25. Don't use negative words: time, work, read, effort, wait, drive...

26. Use only positive words that create energy: easy, fast, fun, effective and affordable.

27. Use an ad agency if they can work with your budget – they know all the tricks, write good copy and can get you the best pricing. They will save you time, money and give you the best chance for success.

28. If you can't use an agency, buy Fred's *Make Money with Radio* marketing three pack that will explain how to advertise on the radio.

29. If you place your own commercials, ask for the first at break and not be buried in the pod or you'll be lost.

30. You must be positioned as the most prominent dentist in a certain niche, technique or area.

31. Barter your dentistry services for free radio time.

32. Do you think if someone like the authors of this book were to supply you with TV, radio and

print advertisements that featured a celebrity spokesperson that you could run in your market and brand your practice it would blow away all competition?

33. Summation: The more consistently you advertise the more patients you will get. The less consistently you advertise the fewer patients you will get. Frequency equals trust and trust equals response.

Fred Catona
1-800-65-ADVERTISE (1 -800-652-3837)

About The Author ...

Fred Catona- is the BILLION-DOLLAR-MAN. He's the only marketer in history to take a startup from zero to $1 billion in sales in just eighteen months. After doing that with PRICELINE.COM, he went on to market and build another billion-dollar brand, FREECREDITREPORT.COM. He is one of the most accomplished and successful marketers on record in his category, Direct Response Marketing. Fred is best known for implementing marketing strategies utilizing celebrity-driven, direct-response advertising. He has also been featured in over one-hundred TV, radio, magazine and online media outlets.

Chapter 10

Write a Book and Become a Celebrity

By Nina Hershberger,

Success is not a magic bullet. It isn't doing any one thing. It's doing a hundred things just like Jerry and the other authors have shared in this book. However, if there's any one thing that can take you instantly to another level – to be known as the celebrity dentist in your local market – it's by writing a book, and then another, and then another.

"But I don't have time."

"I'm not a good writer."

Both are normal and valid reactions to the suggestion of writing a book.

What you may not know is that a large portion of books out there were written by ghostwriters and then just fine-tuned by the actual author. It is a quicker and easier way.

Having your own book is like having a salesperson working for you twenty-four hours a day, seven days a week. That salesperson says the same thing every time – just how you scripted it.

One of my favorite things to do with your book is to give copies of it to your referral sources and let them hand it out free.

Let me explain.

My mother thinks she wants two dental implants but doesn't know much about them, how much they cost, what the process is, etc. Her GP does not do implants so he suggested a couple of oral surgeons that she could go to.

What if my mother lived in your community and you had written the book *"What Every Person Needs to Know about Dental Implants?* "AND you had provided her dentist with copies of your book he/she could hand out to their patients?

- Do you think there is any chance you might be the dentist who gets a lot more referrals than someone else does just because you wrote the book?

- How much more informed and presold do you think my mother would be?

I think you get the idea. The book is your twenty-four-hour salesperson.

Earlier, I talked about having more than one book. Ideally, you should have a general book and one for every niche in your practice.

Hiring a ghostwriter to write any one of these books could cost up to $20,000+.

An easier, lower cost option is to license already written content for each of the books and get a protected territory so no other dentist in your area could have the same book.

Once you're an author you can

1. *Host a book signing event at your office*
2. *Display all your books in your waiting room*
3. *Ask staff members to hand out the book to their family & friends*
4. *Mail a copy to all local media (we'll give you a press release to use) and become their local dental expert when they need one for a story*
5. *Mail a copy to local groups / clubs and offer to speak for them and give each of the attendees a book*
6. *Hand out wherever you exhibit*
7. *Offer it FREE on your website*
8. *Provide copies to your vendors*
9. *Provide copies to your banker*
10. *Send as thank you to your best customers*
11. *Provide copies to all your referral sources*
12. *Hand it out as your "business card"*
13. *Provide some to your local library to put on their shelf*
14. *Use in your "Trust Box" for positioning*
15. *Create posts on social media with the image of your book*
16. *Tweet about your new book on Twitter*
17. *Add an image of your book on your Pinterest pin boards.*
18. *Blog about your new book*
19. *Email to your list about your new book*
20. *Talk about it in your email signature*

Nina Hershberger
CEO and Director of Results
Megabucks Marketing, Inc.
574-320-2522
nina@megabucksmarketing.com

About The Author...

Nina Hershberger *has been in marketing throughout her three-decade professional career—even when her job description said otherwise. After earning a marketing degree from Indiana University, she worked in positions as diverse as Director of Output Services for financial company The Associates and in Procurement for the University Notre Dame. A born marketer, Hershberger added value to her organizations by initiating ideas that increased sales by hundreds of thousands of dollars (and in some cases, millions), added profitable new business services, and raised the companies' profiles.*

In 2006, Hershberger launched Megabucks Marketing to leverage her innovative ideas into concrete results for clients. Her specialty? Leading companies away from the popular but ineffective "cold call, hope, and wait" approach. Thanks to years of experience in the direct mail industry, Hershberger had developed the ability to analyze a client's unique market position and customize ideas to boost their success. One of her specialties is turning local business owners into celebrities by helping them become an author.

Chapter 11

How to Clone Yourself in Your Marketing

By Loren Smith

Would I date a girl without an iPhone? Maybe, but she probably wouldn't like me as much. I'll explain. I'm a single guy. I guess I will be until I find that one special girl. Anyway, until then I date. My goal in dating is to get to know someone and have fun while they get to know me too. These days we text, call, use Facebook, send pictures, audio and video to communicate. I actually have a lot of fun doing this. One of the girls I was dating liked when I would send her random videos of stupid goofy stuff I would do. She thought I was funny and I had a lot of fun doing it. After doing this for a while, I realized that I kept some variety in the relationship by not always using the same way to communicate. It kept her from getting bored. If she didn't have an iPhone, I wouldn't have been able to communicate in so many ways. There are more "smart phones" now than there were at the time, so it's a little easier if they don't have an iPhone.

If you haven't heard it before, marketing can be much like dating. You wouldn't ask someone to marry you on the first date would you? It's a process. Step by step. Making a promise, then coming through with what you promised, then making a promise, etc. You get it.

Before the Internet came around things were much simpler. If you advertised, you had three options: Newspaper, radio or TV. You could call, send a letter or stop by someone's house to follow up. These days, there's online and offline advertising, social media, billboards, and much, much more. You can follow up with email, text, automated phone calls, etc. Overwhelmed yet?
Let's take a step back for a second and apply it to dentistry. You're "dating" your patients. Not really, of course, but you are developing relationships with them. What are the steps that need to be taken? What media will you use to get the message across? Consider these seven basic steps:

1. Call the office or fill out a web form on your website

2. Set an appointment
3. Attend the appointment
4. Accept and schedule treatment
5. Pay for treatment
6. Come back for treatment and future appointments
7. Refer friends and family

Now, take the first and second steps, for example. What can you do to get a future patient that calls to set an actual appointment? Answer the phone when they call? Be friendly on the phone? Have convenient appointments available? Those are just a few things. Each step in the process requires some new information to be shared and understood, and each step can use a variety of media.

In thinking through the process of getting and converting more patients, we've created a system. Every successful business is based on systems. Every scalable business is based on systems. One of the most valuable assets a business has is its systems. Systems make it easier for the staff to do their job and they build trust and consistency with patients. McDonald's understands this very well. We can all agree that the quality of McDonald's product isn't the highest, so why are they so successful? Consistency. I know that every time I go to McDonald's I can expect the same experience. A pretty clean restaurant, my order comes fast and my food tastes the same as the last time. Systems just like at McDonald's are essential to your practice's success.

When implementing systems, every practice needs to consider the resources they have to make it actually happen. You have four main resources:

1. Staff
2. Doctor
3. Patients
4. Software and Hardware

Each of these resources can be used to make your marketing happen, but only software and hardware will help you make these processes <u>personal and automatic</u> without human error.

Most practices I see have some form of practice management software. This could be Dentrix, Open Dental, Eagle soft or others. Many of these practices also have some type of additional software to remind people of their appointments, send emails, text etc. Both of these systems are great, but usually aren't used to their full capabilities. Many practices are spending more money using staff time or missing opportunities that these systems are made to help with or automate completely.

Are you one of the 80% of practices that only use 20% of the software you've paid for or continue to subscribe to?

If so, there is hope. Before you dive in to the software, first know what you're trying to accomplish. It doesn't do much good to use something just because you have it. In the book "Good to Great," Jim Collins studied companies that went from good to great and identified top companies and how they use technology. They always use technology to accelerate what they're trying to accomplish already. Never use technology just because it's there.

In the years of implementing software and helping practices be more efficient, the one major problem I see repeatedly is *trying to make a system too complex, too soon.* Just focus on the one to three major opportunities at first. Make sure those are working first and continue to improve your systems. Over time, you will build a very valuable asset and marketing machine.

If we could treat all of our patients and future patients with the personal attention it takes to court someone, we would have stronger relationships built on trust, which would mean more patients accepting treatment and more referrals. Implementing systems and personalized automation is the key to scale our relationships with our patients.

Would you like some helpful resources to bring everything together? Just visit www.toponedentist.com/jerrybook to request an 11"x17" visual diagram example of what a marketing automation plan looks like and over three-hundred marketing ideas to help you convert more patients.

In case you want to know more about Loren, he is a fresh, enthusiastic young dental marketing consultant who helps dental practices grow through technology and systems. He has worked with many practices throughout the country and strives to help dental practices rise to the top 1%.As a speaker, Loren has appeared with some of the most successful dental marketing "gurus" out there. He loves adrenaline and playing traditional and extreme sports. He also enjoys spending time with his young daughter. Loren lives in Arizona.

Chapter 12

How a Small-Town Dentist in Rural America Generated 549 New Patients From a Three-Hour Event Without Any Marketing!

By Darold D. Opp, DDS

D oes generating 549 new patients from a patient appreciation event sound too good to be true? The main author of this book, Jerry A. Jones, the best marketer in dentistry, touted this success story as "the non-marketing marketing wonder of dentistry!" during his 2013 Dental Office: IMPOSSIBLE dental marketing extravaganza held in Scottsdale, Arizona.

Before we delve into this marketing wonder, let me introduce myself. My name is Dr. Darold Opp and I practice family dentistry in Aberdeen, South Dakota. I live in rural America. I am an average dental clinician. I have a great team, and we have a unique business model. My collections in 2011, 2012, and 2013, during one of the most challenging economies in history, averaged over $3.3 million—$1.3 million in hygiene and $2 million in restorative dentistry. Here is where it gets really interesting. I do not do any of the following procedures: oral surgery including implants, orthodontia, sedation, sleep apnea, TMJ, dentures, full mouth crown and bridge, and upper molar endodontics. A number of dentists at Jerry's event, where I was a featured speaker, asked me, "What is your secret?"

My simple and honest answer? A patient appreciation event! But not just any event, mind you. Our SmilePalooza celebration is so unique that my local newspaper called it "South Dakota's Version of Disney World."

Our event has grown each year, and so have our results. In 2010, we generated 147 new patients and $165,588 in direct revenue. In 2011, 172 new patients and $181,425 in revenue. In 2012, 230 new patients and $206,116 in revenue. In 2013, we created a customized pre-event and post-event marketing campaign for the first time, and our numbers skyrocketed: 232 new patients and $397,594in annual revenue with a lifetime value of $1,160,000. All accomplished with our three-hour SmilePalooza event.

Here is the crazy part: We began SmilePalooza in 2008 with no intention of it being a new patient magnet. My hope and desire was to create a simple appreciation day for my own patients. However, when you live in a small community and have an event in a public venue, it is extremely hard not to open the day to everyone. Hesitantly, that is what we did, and our first-year attendance was eye-popping. We were expecting three-hundred people, and more than three-thousand attended. We had ordered nine-hundred hot dogs, and we ran out in the first hour. We were frantic, to say the least!

Hot dog shortages aside, our inaugural event was a resounding success. We registered 850 children that first year and stopped counting because we ran out of registration stickers. Of those 850 kids, 87% were not our patients, so we realized that opening our event to the public was a great idea after all. SmilePalooza was truly a serendipitous new patient magnet. We did not create any post-event marketing with offers to entice attendees to come to our office until 2013. We know at least 549 new patients came unsolicited during 2010-2012. We failed to track adequately in 2008 and 2009, so our new patient numbers actually far exceeded the 549 we counted.

After our 2008 event, we saw a surge of families come into our office stating that SmilePalooza was their main referral source. We couldn't believe this was happening simply because of a three-hour event, so we decided to host another event the following year, thinking we would "debunk" what had happened in 2008. We were in for another surprise. More than four-thousand people attended in 2009, and the kid count was even higher than in 2008.

You may wonder how reciprocation relates to marketing. Robert B. Cialdini, Ph.D., the foremost expert on social psychology in the world, has written a classic book entitled "Influence: The Psychology of Persuasion." In this book, he writes about six principles of influence that permeate every society. The first principle is reciprocation: If you do a kindness for another, they will feel an obligation to return the favor. The incredible success of SmilePalooza in securing new patients was simply the principle of influence at work. And work it did!

So, what makes SmilePalooza such a unique event? First, no one else is doing one similar. When we began thinking about having an appreciation event for our patients, I did exhaustive research offline and online about how to market events like this and I came up empty. I could not find anything like it outside or inside dentistry. That was frustrating. How in the world would I even begin to try planning such an endeavor? However, as they say in business, either you are a pioneer who paves the way or you are a settler who reaps the efforts of others. We weren't given a choice. We had to be pioneers. Our long history of working with children in the office and creating innovative ideas that give us staying power in the community was in our favor. We already knew what kids and their families enjoy.

Therefore, we created SmilePalooza to be a one-of-a-kind, fun-filled family extravaganza. Imagine an afternoon in the park where four-thousand people gather to see superheroes and Disney princesses come to life, the Tooth Fairy and Tooth Man welcome in old and new friends, multiple inflatable bounce houses, twenty-foot-tall walking puppets roaming the park, and the world's largest bubble tower filling the sky. In addition, we feature fire trucks, clowns, circus animals, live music, dance contests, horse races, celebrities on stage, crazy activities for all ages, shirt cannons, snacks and drinks, and tons of prizes. And the best part—all the laughter, all the screams of joy, all the pictures, and all the family memories are FREE! Google "SmilePalooza 2014" and see for yourself why it has become the #1 free kids' event in dentistry.

One of the rewards of SmilePalooza has already been discussed: new patients. That is very significant! It is no secret that in 2008 the economy went south in a big way. Roger P. Levin, DDS, a well-recognized dental consultant, wrote in the May/June 2013 *Dental Business Review* that a shocking 75 percent of practices had declined in the preceding four years, not only in income but in new patient numbers as well.

In the same newsletter, a roundtable of practice analysts was asked to name the #1 area of concern in the dental practice. They all echoed the same thing: having trouble filling hygiene schedules. My current dental consultant, Mike Abernathy, DDS, wrote in his new book, "The Super General Dental Practice," that the economic downturn of 2008 has drastically changed the business of dentistry and it may never be the same again. Dr. Abernathy goes on to say that we need to be very creative and innovative about the type of dental services we offer, and we must do everything in our power to keep satisfied patients in our practice and to find new ways to create a competitive advantage.

Speaking of competitive advantage, if I asked you what sets you apart from the dental practice next door or down the street, what would your answer be? In my small rural community of 26,000, there are eighteen dentists. For twenty-four years of my dental career, I was frustrated trying to separate myself from the crowd. In the consumer's mind, which is the only perception that really matters, I was no different from the guy next door. Look at any yellow pages ad or, better yet, any website, and you will be hard-pressed to decide what differentiates doctor A from doctor B.

SmilePalooza was truly serendipitous, not only because it has generated hundreds of new patients over the past six years, but also because it has given us a unique competitive advantage that has placed my office into the top "mental real estate" of the moms in my community. Why is that so important? Moms schedule 92% of all dental appointments.

Sally Hogshead in her book "Fascinate: Your 7 Triggers to Persuasion and Captivation" writes about a study in which more than one-thousand people were asked, "What is your#1 fascination in life?" Ninety-six percent responded with "my children."

For any family dentist reading those words, this should be an "aha!" moment. The incredible success of SmilePalooza was orchestrated, in part, by the planning that my team leader and I did, but as Dr. Cialdini revealed in his research on the principles of influence, we were fortunate to target the two most critical pieces of our event's success, moms and their children.

While increasing patient numbers and prospective income was the first reward from our event, there were so many more than we ever anticipated. For example, what business, including dentistry, would turn away free publicity? For six years running, our local newspaper has covered SmilePalooza as a news story, complete with eye-catching photographs and the reporter's commentary. Having our story become one of the top views of the day and remain in the top ten researched for several days after the event was invaluable. The headline "South Dakota's Version of Disney World" would have cost thousands of dollars to buy as ad space, so the free price tag made it priceless!

Increased name recognition in the community helps place you and your practice into an additional position of influence, something that Dr. Cialdini calls social proof/authority.

In 2010, our practice won the prestigious ABBY award, which is the highest honor for community involvement in our city. No other dentist has won the award in its twenty-year history, and we were blessed to overcome all odds, coming in ahead of 3M, a company of 750 employees, and Avera Health, Aberdeen's largest employer, with a team of more than1,300. Not a bad accomplishment for an office of ten!

- In 2012, we were awarded The Hometown Hero award for our commitment to SmilePalooza and the numerous other projects we undertake to better our community. I say these things not to impress you but to impress upon you that anyone can accomplish similar things, if not more, simply by creating a niche that is unique.

- In 2013, I concluded that if we wanted to take our SmilePalooza event to the next level, then we needed to leverage ourselves through the power of networking. Our positive reputation in the community had grown, and it had caught the attention of other businesses, allowing us to garner sponsorships for our event. Through a simple, well-crafted appeal letter, we raised over $19,000 in cash donations and in-kind gifts, eliminating all of our hard costs for SmilePalooza. We were able to generate $397,594in new patient revenue with minimal or no financial costs of our own. Who wouldn't like that return on investment? And there's more! Sponsorships also allowed us to expand our influence into our sponsors 'networks when they personally invited their clients to the event, leveraging even more "dental ambassadors" for SmilePalooza for years to come.

Now we are adding another feature to SmilePalooza, and it's one that has us extremely excited. Make-A-Wish®, the charitable foundation that grants wishes to children who are sick, is becoming actively involved in pre-promotion as well as participating in the event itself. Considering our focus on making a difference for moms and their children, collaborating with this charity makes all the sense in the world. In addition, here is another piece of information that I find interesting: 68% of moms prefer to go to a dentist who is committed to a cause. Interesting data! Make-A-Wish includes references to our partnership on all its social media sites and is providing ongoing promotions up to the day of the event. Can you ever have enough people singing your praises? Not in today's economy!

Another new feature relates to our registration process on the day of the event. We obviously give people the opportunity to preregister on a SmilePalooza website prior to the event, but the vast majority of families sign in on site. New technology has allowed us to instantly merge attendees' names into a database that immediately starts our marketing program the second they hit the submit button. Strike while the iron is hot! In addition, the attendees have the opportunity to sign up for a free computer-based loyalty program that has weekly interactive contests, free games, and other goodies that allow us another opportunity to stay engaged with potential new patients throughout the course of the twelve months leading up to the next year's event.

We have created an extensive marketing program that keeps SmilePalooza actively working throughout the year. Through scripted emails, recorded radio ads, follow-up postcards and personalized thank-you notes, we are able to reach a "warm" lead (someone who has attended our event) with our marketing efforts. One cannot overestimate the importance of repeated contacts to the same leads. A commonly accepted marketing principle is that it takes as many as seven positive touches to get a prospect to become a buyer. If the event is our first impression with an attendee, every contact beyond that moves us one step closer to success.

By now, you may want to ask me, "How in the world does the average dentist attempt to accomplish everything you have mentioned?" It is all about the power of SYSTEM (Save-Your-Self-Time-Energy-Money). Since we were the pioneers of this type of event marketing, you can become the settler who reaps the rewards of all our heavy lifting. In the introduction, I mentioned the Dental Office: IMPOSSIBLE marketing seminar.

Many of the top marketers in dentistry presented at this meeting, and it was there that the SmilePalooza Event-In-A-Box coaching program was shared for the first time. Clients are already on board, and excitement continues to grow for those who want to create the #1 niche for attracting moms and their children to their practices. We have created an informative and free webinar at www.3HourFamilyDentalMarketing.com that will take you systematically through all the details of our program. If your interest goes beyond the webinar, you will have the opportunity for a free consultation with me to answer your questions and to discover if we can team together to further your success in dentistry.

SmilePalooza may be only one small hinge of your marketing strategy, but as you have seen from the results, it swings a BIG REVENUE DOOR!

Here's to our continued success in the best profession in the world!

[The co-author of this book, Jerry A. Jones, contributed copy and strategy for Dr. Opp's campaigns, all of which have been featured and referred to in an internationally released, best-selling program titled, *The Ultimate No B.S. Referral Machine.*]

About The Author...

Darold Opp, DDS, *is a family dentist in Aberdeen, S.D., population 26,091. He has a single doctor practice that produces $3.4 million a year without comprehensive crown and bridge, oral surgery, dentures, implant surgery, TMJ, sleep apnea, and sedation dentistry. Dr. Opp went from $500,000 in debt in 2010 to recreating lifetime savings and ready to retire in four years using the strategies in this chapter.*

Chapter 13

The Internet from 50,000 Feet

By Matt Prados

Disclaimer: The following chapter is an honest look at the Internet marketing industry as a whole. I will tell it as I see it. You can believe me or not, but this was written for you. I will not sugar coat it, I will call out a few other companies. As I pull the covers back, giving you a good look at the industry, I hope you will use this information to make better choices in your online marketing moving forward.

Internet Marketing Sales Reps Are ~~Honest~~ People

So first, let me say that I actually love sales people. I believe that the world turns because sales people sell. Without selling, there is no business. To think otherwise is just ridiculous. Having said that, there are good sales people/companies that are not well versed in sales who KNOW what they are selling and how it works while having the prospect's best interests at hand. Then there are BAD sales people/companies that can sell and don't care about the end user at all.

Unfortunately, internet marketing has had its share of sales people/companies that are in the subpar section of this good/bad spectrum. If you are reading this chapter, it's a safe bet that you have tried at least one but probably more like five or six internet marketing companies and, frankly, they lied to your face and you were screwed.

"You can't track that!" – So says nearly every marketing sales rep, ever.

That is the common response of marketing sales reps and advertising companies. This is important because they know that the metrics or stats they give you are a bunch of garbage that simply does not result in you making money. "Perceived value, "is what they call it. I do not believe in perceived value as you cannot pay the bills with perceived value.

Can you just change your services and be an expert in the new category?

Yellow Page ad companies turned website marketing companies are a joke. Think about their board meeting... "We are dying in a media that will become extinct, but we have a big database of businesses that we have sold print advertising to. Now that print is dead what can we do?" Intern raises his hand and says, "We should just change our business from print to digital and keep selling to the same businesses because otherwise we are screwed. And, well, since they do not track results anyway, how hard can real internet marketing be anyway? Let's just make a website and they will pay us just the same." CEO says "Approved!" and so history is made.

Social Media Marketing Is A Lie.

Studies show that social media engagement is dropping from rates of 15% to rates as low as 6% in the last few years alone, and at this rate, will be 0% in two more years. A select few businesses can use social media well: restaurants, clothing companies and, maybe, personal development gurus. C'mon, do you really think your patients want to hear about the latest crown technology? Maybe if you are a children's dentist and you get moms to follow you and you post cute pictures about kids at the dentist and how to get children to have cleaner, stronger teeth you will get some traction.

However, unless they think it is so great to share it, who cares really, because it is not getting you new patients. "Likes" do not equal new patients. They only serve to boost your ego. There is one thing I like social media for, but that will be covered in the section on "Reviews," which can equal new patients but I will cover that in another chapter.

Critical Error: Using more than one company.

This is probably one of the biggest mistakes I see dentists make. Because there are so many companies out there making outrageous claims and calling you on a weekly basis, sometimes you hire more than one company at the same time. The problem lies in having more than one company working on your marketing and one not knowing about the other. This can cause you problems that neither can explain because they do not know the other exists or exactly what they are doing.

Case in point: If you have two companies working on your local listings so you easily appear in local searches for "dentist" and other keywords, you can have duplicate, yet only partially correct listings made. You can have one company work on optimizing one street address that may have a suite number and the other company optimizing without the suite number, or with "Ave" vs. "Avenue," or with a slight variation of your business name, etc. These inconsistencies can have a dramatically negative effect and cause conflict among search engines, which actually end up penalizing you. Or, if two companies have claimed the same Google map listing then Google may not push the updates live from one of the accounts that are trying to "optimize" it.

There Are Only Two, True Options

The truth is you really only have two options. First, hire a full-time person that does this in your office so they know exactly what is happening on every aspect at a cost of $3,000 to $5,000 per month, not including the paid ad expense. Second, hire ONLY one company that handles the entire process from start to finish.

Otherwise, I can pretty much guarantee that you will have cross over where they step on each other's toes and, in the end, you are the one that suffers for it.

Getting Your Website to Rank is ONLY 10% of the work (Conversion Optimization)

So many people only think in terms of rankings: where does my site rank, how fast can you get my site to the top, etc. These are the questions of the untrained internet marketer.

What you need to be asking is: What percent of your unique visitors convert to the exact action you desire? In your case, this metric is calls to your office to schedule an appointment.

This percentage should ideally be 10%. Most of you reading this will find you probably have around a 1% conversion rate, and through redesigning your website and continual testing of its design you can increase this percentage.

The first thing you have to do is build your website right. What does this mean? First, you have to think:

What are my visitors looking for, what do they want? They most likely want to find a dentist that they like and can trust. Does your website address that?

So many people try to sell on technical points like what crown-milling machine you use, or a particular procedure.

You should be selling an experience: how they will feel and what result they will get. I do not consider smile galleries as a selling experience either. If you have one that takes up the entire top of the site with stock photos or even real photos, you are likely turning people away.

Think about the last time you read a brochure. I mean actually looked at it with interest and found something you were looking for. Probably never, with the exception of buying new equipment for your office.

Are you giving website visitors a "mafia offer? "In other words, an offer they cannot refuse. A reason to pick up the phone and call you immediately. "Accepting New Patients" or "Call (888) no offer" are typical offers I see that do nothing to motivate the prospect to call.

Free whitening for life, a free exam and x-rays, free consultation, coupled with a $29 cleaning... these are offers that people are much more likely to call about. You have taken the risk away from them and put it on you. First, make sure you have communicated to them that you understand them and you know what they are going through and how you can help them.

WIIFM – What's in it for me? This is what is going through people's heads. You have to enter the conversation that the person is already having in their head and move it to the thing you want them to do, all the while making them think it was their idea.

They do not want all your social media profile icons. They do not likely care about "free Wi-Fi." If you were voted the best dentist, *that* is something they will likely want to know. If you have great reviews, those are something people will DEFINITELY want to see. (More on that in a little bit.)

You have to communicate to them in more than one media. You should have text, images and video. You will want NOT to overdo it with communication or data overload. Give them enough to want to call you.

Get people to stay on your site!

You'll want to make your site "sticky." Now, I don't mean page views here. You see page views for a local site like a dental site usually means that the person was not successfully sold on the home page. Time on site is more what I mean – keeping them on your site long enough to find what they need to trust and like you enough to pick up the phone.

Keep It Fresh.

The Internet is still just a teenager. Google was actually officially born in as a corporation and got funding on my son's birthday, the actual day he was born, September 4, 1998. Websites look very different to what they looked like two years ago or even last year. Make sure your site is always innovative. I do not suggest buying a high-dollar website. I suggest getting a company that will constantly update your website as website standards change.

The current big question: Is your site mobile optimized? Better yet, is it responsive? Meaning that it shows differently depending on the device it is being viewed on. This is not nearly as important as standard conversion optimization talked about above, but it is useful.

Are you updating your content, blogging and getting new reviews (dates are shown on reviews)?These are all things that visitors may not know they are looking at or for but they give an impression of you based on your website freshness.

Getting people to visit your website.

Most website owners fixate on visitors and rankings, so I will not spend too much time here, except to demonstrate further that if you have not yet done conversion optimization on your website and are only getting 1% conversion, even with great rankings driving traffic to your site, you will get ten calls. Conversion of visitors to callers is key.

A note about website traffic: For a local dental office, three- to five-hundred visitors from your area per month would be a lot of visitors.

If you are able to get your site converting at 10% and with bad rankings, getting one-hundred visitors per month (25-35% of what's likely available) you would get those same ten calls.

If you add good rankings on top of good conversion optimization, where you are getting three- to five-hundred visitors per month with a 10% conversion rate, you could be getting thirty to fifty calls per month.

I think you are starting to get the point, but one last thing: Search terms, those words entered into search engines by prospective patients, are not all created equal. Some terms have an informational twist or intention, and the good ones have a buying intention. You only really care about the buying intention to start. Once you have those down, you can add the informational type searches, and you may get some to conversion to buyers, but focus on the buying intention for fastest and best results.

If you would like a FREE website review, I would be happy to help you. Go to www.gotchalocal.com/bookdeal for a FREE website review.

Customer Reviews

This topic could be a chapter all by itself. Reviews are the new social proof and, really, a social currency. In years past, you would see sites with BBB logos and other "trust" logos that people used to sway the visitors that their website was a trustworthy site.

However, reviews are now the only real indicator. So few businesses have embraced getting reviews because, oftentimes, their staff members tell them how "hard" it is to get reviews.

I will tell you how easy it actually is. You already pay your front desk folks to check in and check out your patients, right? When they are leaving simply have your front desk person do this:

Your staff: "How was your visit?"

Patient: "Great!" (If you are any good at what you do)

Your staff: "Excellent, would you mind giving us a good review?"

Patient: "Sure"

Your staff: "Thanks do you have a Google account, Yelp account, Yahoo account or something else?"

Patient: "Tells which site"

Your staff: "Here is a flier that tells you where to go and what to do to leave a review on _____."

Then, have the front desk person email this patient the directions with a link to the site to leave the review.

Another way to get reviews is to email your patients. But you have to be careful on this one. Too many reviews too fast can cause sites like Google and Yelp to flag, filter or remove your reviews. Most of them have their sites terms of service, which say that they are not okay with your soliciting reviews. All of them say that you cannot compensate for reviews.

However, this is the real world and with your business making money at stake, you have competition, so you need to make things happen if you want to survive, let alone thrive. So, yes, I say ask for them, ask for them via email, but do it smart and smart is NOT all at once. To help with this,www.messagemetric.com actually allows you to send a bulk email in portions every day. This will then make your reviews come in at a normal and acceptable rate.

Another way to get reviews is to send postcards or letters to patients and ask for reviews. Again, I would drip them out over time, not all at once.

If you would like scripts for these emails and design ideas for the postcards go to www.messagemetric.com/scripts and I will give you the scripts and design ideas for at no charge.

The bottom line is you are asking for reviews whether via one-on-one conversations, via email, or via direct mail. It is just communication and NOT hard.

Think about how many reviews you have now. A few, maybe a dozen, if you are lucky. If for the last five years you got one review per week, you would have 260 reviews! Even if you lost half because Google and Yelp suck and filter or flag them, you would still have 130, which is ten-times what you have now.

The Internet is not going away. Reviews are going to have equity forever, even when you want to sell your practice! The more reviews you have will help you sell your practice for more money. Reviews are literally money in the bank.

Studies show that prospects TRUST reviews almost as much as a referral from a friend. What is your favorite type of new patient? A referral, right? This is the next best thing.

Speaking of referrals, the one thing I like social media for is getting existing patients to post to THEIR Facebook timeline. Have them post that they are visiting your office and how great it is. This is then seen by their friends, many of whom are local to them and to you and some of whom may need the same service you just did for their friend and, boom, you could get a referral from social media.

How many times can you get a patient to post for you? Have a computer station in your reception area for checking and posting to social media sites. Ask for Facebook check-ins. Yes, there are others: Foursquare, Twitter, etc., but Facebook will get you the most traction with this strategy.

Paying For Website Visitors

If you are not paying for visitors to go to your site, you are leaving money on the table.

Some people will only click on organic or free listings, but many *will* click paid ads and some will never search for you but will click your ad if it is stuck in front of them at the right time.

These ads are paid for based on either number of impressions or number of clicks. You can play with both formats and see which works best for you in your area, with your niche.

Here is a list of many places you can and should buy traffic from:

Google Ads – Google has search ads, display ads and retargeting ads. Search ads are when someone types in "dentist your town" and your ad shows. Display are the ads on others websites that visitors see because they visited a website that sells ad space to Google. Retargeting is when someone has visited your site, your site gave him or her a cookie and Google knows to show your ad to him or her based on that. Search is the best tool for you as a dentist. Display and retargeting will not likely do much for you. Google gets about 70% of all search traffic. You must use Google AdWords!

Facebook Ads – Facebook is like a coffee shop. People are there and hanging out and not really looking for you but, if one of their friends mentions you, then you are in the conversation. Alternatively, if you have an ad show and if your ad shows that a friend likes you, then that is almost as good. This is a definite source of traffic to experiment with.

Bing/Yahoo Ads – These two are both served off the same platform and are Google search-type ads, but only appear on Yahoo and Bing search engines. I do like Google's targeting options better than Bing/Yahoo. These two search engines only get about 30% of all search traffic.

Yelp Ads – This is probably the worst investment for paid ads for a website in 98% of the cases. These ads are only shown on Yelp's site and they usually cost two- to three- times what a click on Google costs. Yelp always shows other competitors listings on your listing and based on my own personal testing, these have a very low conversion rate and return on investment is usually poor. Occasionally, I hear someone that did well, but, because they lock you in for twelve months, the risk is almost never worth the reward and should only be used after you are winning on all other types of paid ads.

Retargeting – As mentioned earlier, this can be done via Google, but worth mentioning are other companies that you can use besides Google. I have tried a few and some will do better than others in different areas will.

Banner Ads – These have been around almost as long as the Internet itself. This is just an image ad showing on a website with little targeting options.

Yodle and Reach Local are companies that specialize in paid advertising models but are not in your best interest, in my opinion. And here's why: They are resellers of Google ad clicks. Google charges $2 and these companies charge you $3 or $4 for the same click. Therefore, there is a ton of wasted money on clicks so they can make their numbers. Moreover, they are so big that when they hire reps and tell them to study their manuals, these reps suddenly become "experts" at paid search. They are not experts. So how knowledgeable is the person spending your money, really?

Let's get real for a moment.

If your marketing campaigns are not getting you NEW Patients, then STOP doing them and find campaigns that do.

Stop looking at page views, keyword reports for terms that no one ever searches, impressions or even clicks, as these can be manipulated to "look" good, but they result in NOTHING.

Primarily, you can and should focus on making your phone ring and tracking the calls. If you track phone calls, record them, sort them by services offered, advertising source and whether they resulted in a new patient scheduling or not. Then, and only then, should you start to look at the other metrics like clicks, unique visitors, page views, etc.

You can track calls from any source whether in print or online. Your site can be made to show a different phone number based on how people get to the site and therefore tell you what advertising they came from.

I built a platform for business owners to be able to track their calls easily and I want to give you a FREE TRIAL to it. If you want to improve your marketing return on investment, then you can do it by making your advertising companies get honest about results.

For the FREE trial go to

www.MessageMetric.com/bookdeal

Please start tracking your results.

About The Author...

Matt Prados *is a sales and marketing veteran with over
2 decades in the trenches of selling. Avid student of
business, sales and direct marketing and a seminar
junkie he has studied under every Guru in these
fields. He has taken this information, tested it, reorganized it,
customized it and automated it and reduced it to what works in
marketing a successful practice online. No fluff just what works. He
shares this information on his blog, website, articles and the chapter in
this book. He is currently working on his own book, running a very
successful online marketing agency, launching a call tracking company
and coaching his son's soccer team while living his dream with his
beautiful wife of 17 years and their 2 sons in Southern California.*

Chapter 14

The Secret to Getting New Referrals

By Jon Keel
with Elysse Curry
5 Star Strategic Results, LLC

D o you agree with this statement? *"Your practice is dependent upon your reputation and your good reputation leads to more referrals, and more referrals leads to more patients and* revenue."

The answer is obvious.

The good news is that there are two types of referrals; one you're quite familiar with and one that, if you understand its power, can provide new patients to you, as this chapter title says, all on autopilot.

The first type of referral, *Personal Referrals*, you know very well. Hopefully, you have an active *Personal Referral* plan in place. If you've been in practice for more than several years, you understand its power.

(Image 1)

Personal Referrals

- "Here's someone you should see"
- Private
- One to One
- Offline (in person)
- Dependent upon personal contact – time and place dependent

Personal referrals result, for example, from one of your existing patients responding, perhaps to a question from a friend, family member or coworker, about where to find a good dentist. "Here's someone you should see" are golden words to you. By definition, Personal Referrals are private, occur during a one-to-one conversation, and are totally time and place dependent.

The second type of referrals we call *Public Referrals©*. Understanding and implementing a *Public Referrals©* system cannot only bring you new patients on autopilot, but it can give you a long-term sustainable competitive advantage in your local market place.

(Image 2)

Personal Referrals	Public Referrals ©
• "Here's someone you should see"	• Internet Reviews
• Private	• Public
• One to One	• One To Many
• Offline (in person)	• Online
• Dependent upon personal contact – time and place dependent	• Available 24 x 7 – continually visible

Public Referrals© are commonly called internet reviews, but using this terminology downplays their significance. Compared to *Personal Referrals, Public Referrals©* are in public view, online, but most importantly are available 24 x 7 instead of being time and place dependent.

Sometimes dentists will ask, "Which should I use?" My response, "Do both, and understand their overwhelming power when you use them together." In today's environment, if you understand your prospective patients' behavior, you'll become totally committed to using them both.

Let me explain.

Let's followup on the example I noted above, where a prospective patient asks one of your patients where he or she can find a good dentist. Because you've done such a good job of implementing a *Personal Referrals* program, your patient tells them about you.

What's the first thing the prospective patient will do?

What would you do if you were the prospective patient?

Many people to whom I've asked that question respond, "Well, I'd check them out online." And that's what the most recent research shows.

My friend David Sprague of Real Strategic, Inc., recently commissioned an independent research study focusing on referral behavior. Some of the results are astounding.

In response to the question, "What do you do after being referred a business?" here's what people said:

- 87% search online to find the company information
- 4% dial 411 to find the company information
- 6% use a phone book to find the company information
- 2% do something else

Look at those figures again. *Almost nine out of ten people go online after they've been given an offline referral.*

It should be obvious that you want to get very good (if you're not already) at implementing both *Personal Referrals* and *Public Referrals*© in your practice.

Then, and I believe this is the more significant finding of the research, in response to the question, "What do you do first when you search online for a business?" the respondents said:

- 52% look for online reviews and ratings
- 35% look for the website and contact information
- 13% look up social media pages

Not to jump to the end of the story, but I'll come back to these results as they are important in the next chapter.

Do you see how *Personal Referrals* and *Public Referrals*© are closely intertwined? Today, they meld in with your prospective patients' natural behavior.

Why Is This More Important Today?

Knowing what your prospective patients are doing when they find out about your practice, what will they find when they search online for you?

Do you have negative reviews?

Almost as badly, do you have no reviews?

Or, do you have a large number of **5 Star** reviews online?

And are your existing **5 Star** reviews spread in multiple places across the Internet (tying into the second part of the above research)?

Before we get into answering these questions, here's some background information.

In mid-2012, Google made major changes that overnight affected eighty-million local businesses worldwide. Briefly, Google now shows your Online Reputation (the number of *Public Referrals*© you have), not only in your local Google listing, but for any of up to twenty review websites (Yelp, Insider Pages, Merchant Circle, etc.)
A friend of mine says that your Online Reputation is now out there "in front of God and everybody."

Four major "game changers" for local businesses have occurred because of these changes.

Here's Game Changer #1:

(Image 3)

As of June 2012, when you type in any company name and a city in Google, it reveals the company's reputation. In the above example, I searched for "dentist Cincinnati oh"; I found ███████████ ███████ (for obvious reasons I've blacked out the name of the practice) ranked near the top. I then typed in "███████████████████ Cincinnati" into Google and got the above results.

You'll note that, on the plus side, this practice has eleven Google reviews. On the negative side, and this is a big negative, it has a 2.9 out of 5 stars reputation rating. This is incredibly poor. The bottom line is that this practice does not have a good reputation.

Therefore, anyone actually searching for them, maybe even just to get directions, is going to type in their name and the city to find some more information. Ask yourself if you would go any further or would you move on to find a dentist with a higher reputation rating.

Moving On To Game Changer #2:

As a local businessperson, you're interested in having good visibility online. In fact, this was our major focus for the first four years we were involved in helping local businesses increase the numbers of their new customers, clients or patients.

It was all about ranking and position, using SEO, Google Local marketing, etc., with a secondary focus on reputation.

(Image 4)

That is the wrong approach after Google's June 2012 changes. As a sidelight, it brought about a 180° change in focus in our business model, but one that was necessary.

As one of our dental members said to me several months ago, "Why would I want to invest time and money in getting my website ranked and good positioning in Google Local, if, when people find me, they find either a bad reputation or no reputation? Let's develop the **5 Star** reputation first."

Very insightful.

Bringing Us to Game Changer #3:

(Image 5)

As noted above, the traditional local online marketing of focusing on ranking doesn't work anymore *if you have bad reviews or no reviews online.*

As the picture below shows, your first priority today needs to be to develop a **5 Star** reputation online and then focus on positioning.

Wrapping Up With Game Changer #4:

Until now, I've discussed the downside of what's occurring with *Local Online Reputation* and *Public Referrals©*.

Let's now take some time reviewing some of the very positive issues regarding the game changers.

(Image 6)

**Reviews Send You Prequalified Presold Customers.
Because Buyers Trust Reviews...
As Much As Personal Recommendations.**

72% Of Buyers Trust Reviews As Much
As Personal Recommendations

About The Author: Myles Anderson is Founder & CEO of BrightLocal.com. BrightLocal

First, reviews send you prequalified, presold customers because "buyers trust reviews as much as personal recommendations." Reviews can be incredibly bad for you if they're bad, but they can be incredibly good for you if they're really good (think **5 Star**).

As the above information from Myles Anderson of Bright Local shows, 72% of buyers trust reviews as much as personal recommendations. I've recently heard that a recent update (not yet published) increases this figure to 78%.

Would you rather create your marketing plan for people that don't know you, don't like you, don't trust you and always are worried about price? Or would you rather create a marketing plan with people that know you, people that like you, people that trust you... and they feel that way because they're all referrals (either personal or public)?

Of course, you would want to create a referral marketing plan.

For the first time, the recent Google changes have allowed your online marketing using *Public Referrals©* to be just as powerful as traditional personal referrals marketing.

This is such a big game changer, I'd like to take it a little deeper.

A recent report from Nielsen, one of the most respected companies in tracking advertising results, addresses this point. Nielsen asked the question, "To what extent do you trust different forms of advertising; which are the most important things that you trust?"

(Image 7)

To what extent do you trust the following forms of advertising?

Global Average	Trust Completely/ Somewhat	Don't Trust Much/ At All
Recommendations from people I know	92%	8%
Consumer opinions posted online	70%	30%
Editorial content such as newspaper articles	58%	42%
Branded Websites	58%	42%
Emails I signed up for	50%	50%
Ads on TV	47%	53%
Text ads on mobile phones	29%	71%

Source: Nielsen Global Trust in Advertising Survey, Q3 2011

As you can see, 92% of people trust recommendations from people that they know. But here's the big one. Look at the second line. Seventy percent of people trust opinions based on online reviews.

You can see we have one stat from Bright Local saying 72%. We've have the Nielsen stat of 70%. This is huge!

However, delve into the Nielsen graphic a little more. People actually trust consumer opinions posted online more than an editorial newspaper or article. You could have a newspaper article written about you that is editorial in content and people will not trust that as much as an online review.

All the evidence points to the fact that using *Public Referrals©* as part of your **Reputation Marketing** is the most important marketing that you can do for your practice. So, if you going to do any type of marketing with your practice, it shouldn't start with the type of marketing the people don't trust – TV ads at 47% or e-mail marketing at 50% or even branded website marketing at 58%. It should start with the top two - recommendations from your patients (Personal Referrals), and consumer opinions posted online (*Public Referrals©*, or **Reputation Marketing.**)

Moving along, why are *Public Referrals©* and **Reputation Marketing** so vital to your dental practice?

The graphic below is enlightening.

(Image 8)

This shows that consumers look up an average of ten reviews before making a decision. All of these consumers are online. They're looking for reviews as the research above shows.

More importantly, they're looking at multiple reviews, not just one or two. This information answers the question of "how many reviews do you actually need to be credible?" Seventy percent of consumers trust a business with a minimum of six to ten reviews. If consumers are looking for six reviews and you have six reviews showing then you're in good shape.

Additionally, you are not credible without **5 Star** reviews. Witness the above example from the dentist in Cincinnati; it obviously has a number of reviews with less than **5 Stars**. Without a **5 Star** reputation and a minimum of six reviews, your business just can't be trusted when people actually find you.

This is the difference between your phone ringing and it not ringing. More importantly, this is the difference between your phone not ringing and your competition's phone ringing (if they have more **5 Star** reviews than you do). This is so incredibly important: you want not just a minimum of six reviews but also six **5 Star** reviews, so that when people see your business online, your phone rings.

To add a little "icing on the cake," so to speak, here's a summary of a recent Economic Journal article.

(Image 9)

Although this data had to do with restaurant reservations, it should be obvious that increasing your **5 Star** rating with positive reviews (*Public Referrals*©) will have an impact on your practice.

What Does This Mean To You?

This chapter has given you a new way to look at referrals.

Your Personal Referrals are important. Additionally, *Public Referrals*© are one of the ways your prospective patients will make a decision about whether or not to become your patient.

You need to integrate both types of referrals fully in your practice.

Your *Public Referrals*© "work for you" continuously.

When your prospective patient hears about you, almost 100% will check you out online.

Google's June 2012 changes now display your *Public Referrals*© (reviews) for all to see.

Your prospective patients have a high propensity to believe your *Public Referrals*©.

Increasing the number of your **5 Star** reviews (high rated Public Referrals©) cannot only increase the number of new patients for your practice, but (as we'll get into more detail in the next chapter), give you a decided competitive advantage.

What Is Your Local Online Reputation?

Do you know your local **Online Reputation**?

You can check this out manually or request a complimentary **Local Reputation Report** (see how at the end of this chapter).

Below is an example of a **Local Reputation Report** we ran for the Cincinnati dentist previously mentioned.

The report also shows the actual negative reviews that are posted on the Internet (for obvious reasons we've not shown the reviews here).

As you'll note, this report gives you a snapshot of your local Online Reputation, where you're doing well and where you're not doing so well.

What's Next?

In the next chapter we'll get into the details of the steps you can take to create, market, and manage your Local Online Reputation and create a culture within your practice so that all of your staff is "on the same page" when it comes to maximizing the effect of your *Public Referrals©*

TIME-TESTED SECRETS TO ATTRACT NEW
& RETAIN EXISTING PATIENTS

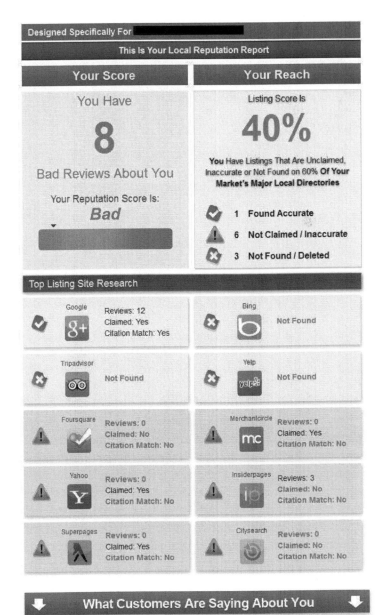

About The Author...

Jon Keel has developed a local and national reputation as a local business online presence and reputation marketing expert, having been actively involved in this arena since 2008. His most recent company, 5 Star Strategic Results, LLC, which he co-founded in 2013, creates 5 star online reputations and then markets those reputations for several hundred local businesses across the U.S.

He co-developed the Xavier University MBA E-Business program, where he taught Online Marketing and E-Commerce for over three years.

He frequently speaks to local, regional, and national audiences. He has written numerous articles and has appeared on several TV news and talk programs.

He co-developed the first pay-per-click search engine bid management software in 2000 and wrote the first book on pay-per-click search engines, "Instant Web Site Traffic" (August, 2001). He also contributed to the best-selling book, "Success Secrets of the Online Marketing Superstars," published in 2005. His most recent book, "Secrets of Peak Performers," which he co-authored with Dan Kennedy, Bill Glazer, and Lee Milteer, was published in April, 2009.

Jon moved to Cincinnati in 1971 as an environmental engineer with the Procter and Gamble Company. He left P&G in 1973 to work for The Henry P. Thompson Company, over a 22-year period becoming the owner and President/CEO, before selling his interest in 1995. He received an MBA from Xavier University in 1987

Chapter 15

You Can Laugh At Not Getting New Patients...If You Follow This Simple Plan

---

By Jon Keel
with Elysse Curry
5 Star Strategic Results, LLC

I n the last chapter we presented the concept of *Public Referrals©* (which some people refer to as internet reviews) and developed the case for your increasing the number of **5 Star** reviews for your practice.

To remind you of the two major benefits:

(1) Almost 90% of your prospective patients are going online to "check you out"; a large number of **5 Star** reviews will increase the probability they will become new patients.

(2) You can create a competitive advantage in your local marketplace if you develop and execute a strategy to increase and market the number of **5 Star** reviews for your practice.

In this chapter, we will take things to the next level by showing you how you can use a relatively simple plan of maximizing the number of patient *Public Referrals©* you get and continually adding to them so that your prospective patients become new patients.

What Is Reputation Marketing?

I previously referred to **Reputation Marketing**. Before I get into the details, let me first make a distinction.

A number of fine companies perform what "reputation management." Reputation management doesn't get your phone ringing. Management is a very defensive or reactive posture. On the other hand, marketing is a very offensive or proactive posture.

In my previous traditional business, we never increased revenue by managing better, but we always increased revenue by marketing better.

How about you?

While a number of people have been doing reputation management for a long time, I believe they don't understand the big game changers that have happened and how today it's all about **Reputation Marketing**. We believe that if you focus only on reputation management, your competitors who understand Reputation Marketing will leave you behind.

Definition: Reputation Marketing is building a 5 Star reputation online and marketing that reputation to get more patients

How Do You Create A Reputation Marketing Strategy?

Do you agree that we hear in words but think in pictures?

Aren't your eyes always drawn more to images that text? I believe that's why Facebook, for example, strongly suggests using images along with text if you do Facebook advertising.

Look at this picture.

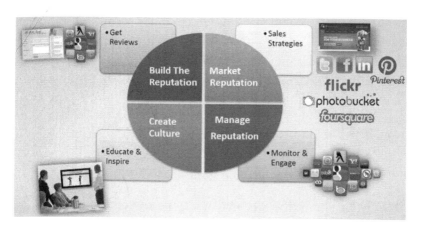

Real Strategic, Inc. All Rights TM

You want to think of your **Reputation Marketing** strategy as a four-part process with very distinct steps that need to be followed in an exact order.

Step 1: Build Your Reputation

It starts with your getting patient **5 Star** reviews. You want to create a system within your practice to have your patients consistently leave reviews in a way that doesn't overtax your staff (they do have other work to do).

Here are several ideas for you:

a. Postcards - create professionally designed review postcards and send them out to your patients inviting them to leave a review – we've found that existing patients love to give **5 Star** reviews.

b. Business cards – create business cards that your staff can pass out to your patients. Having a business card that tells your patients where they can put the review and making it easily accessible is vital for creating a **5 Star** reputation.

c. Email templates - create email templates. Sending email to your patients is an easy way to get reviews, but you actually have to work things a certain way to be able to create a specific type of template that motivates your patients to not only read your email but also take action.

d. Private review page –create a private review page to which your patients can post their reviews. Then, have the completed review feed into a database where it can be used in multiple ways (see the next section for ideas on this).

e. Include a way that your patient can, from within the system, post their review to one of several review websites (e.g., Google, Insider Pages, Merchant Circle, etc.) while ensuring the system doesn't violate IP restriction guidelines from any of these websites.

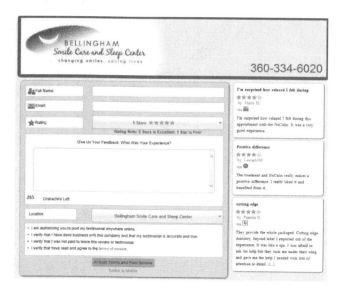

Note the previous patients' reviews on the right side that give the reviewing patient some ideas of what to write.

Here are some ideas on how you could use your private review page – use it in conjunction with your postcards or email templates as the page to which they link; have the page set up on a computer or tablet computer at your front desk where your patients can easily leave their review. The list goes on. We've found that our members continually come up with new ideas on how to use it.

f.   Posting strategy – this is critical. Even if you were to collect reviews for yourself, you can't post your patient reviews directly from your practice location. The reason is that most of the different review sites (e.g., Google) have created an algorithm and filters that delete or "bury" reviews that are posted from the same computer IP network. So that means if you take a few reviews and have your staff post them from your office, they instantly get filtered and even deleted.

This is the advantage of having a private review page. When you have a review page (as discussed above) to collect and filter all your reviews, include a system that gets around review filters. This can be a combination that allows you to dominate and separate yourself from everyone else in your local market. None of your competitors has this.

Step 2: Market Your Reputation

Once you've begun to get your patients' reviews, it's time to begin your reputation marketing process.

Here are some examples:

a. Website marketing – Put your **5 Star** reviews on your website. You know from the previous chapter that 35% of people who are referred to your practice check out your website. As an aside, you can also add the private review page as a separate page on your website as another way to make it easy for your patients to leave reviews.

b. Review websites – although Google is important, what's also necessary is to get your reviews posted across multiple review websites. The previously noted research shows that 52% of people referred to your practice check for your online reviews. This also gives you more breadth of exposure and some say is important in your Google+ Local ranking.

c. Social media marketing – The research noted in the previous chapter shows that 13% of people who are referred to your practice check you out on social media.

Post your written reviews to sites such as Facebook, LinkedIn and Twitter. Although you may not be a regular user of these sites, understand that many of your patients are.

What about images? We know that images (or pictures) draw the eye. Create images of your reviews (and include a call to action with your phone number) and post them to social media image sites such as Facebook, Pinterest, Flickr, etc. Unlike written content on social media sites, images are, in a sense, "memorialized" and have permanence.

NOTE: By combining posting of reviews to your website, review websites and social media, you've covered 100% of the places that your prospective patients go after they've been given a personal referral. Not to overstate, but this is huge.

d. Email marketing – add a **5 Star** review to your signature file in your outbound emails with a link to your private review page. Every email you send will have the review along with a way for the recipient to leave you a review immediately.

e. Video review marketing – some people say that video is the great "unequalizer" in today's online marketing. Face it; we are a TV society. Moreover, Google owns YouTube.

You can use video in two ways.

First, get short (sixty- to ninety-second) video testimonials from your patients. These can be used very effectively on your website and on YouTube.

Next, take the same patient written review you've received and create a short video of the content. Optimizing the video for positioning in

Google can work wonders for getting the reviews to show in normal search.

Step 3: Manage Your Reputation

Although I mentioned earlier that reputation marketing is reactive rather than proactive, reputation management is a part of your overall **Reputation Marketing** plan.

First, you need to ensure that you monitor your online reputation daily.

A number of businesses monitor their branding by using tools like Google Alerts. Unfortunately, Google Alerts and many other tools don't work when it comes to monitoring your reputation. The reason is that these tools only work when someone types in your name or something about your service. Google Alerts searches the entire web for your name or your service.

The problem occurs for this reason. When someone posts a review, they're typically doing it for your business listing on a review website (e.g., Google, Yelp, City Search, etc.) and they never mention your name at all. They post something about you but not your practice name, your name, nor the service. Therefore, you can have all the alerts you want from all these tools but none of them will show your reviews.

You want to have a way to monitors all the major sites on which your business is listed. Every single day you know exactly who posts and what's posted to these sites.

You regularly (we suggest every two to four weeks) want to be able to track how your reputation is increasing online. More importantly, this kind of report is incredible for you, the practice owner, to share with your staff so they know how well they are doing. You want to see both the good reviews and bad reviews in this report. The bad reviews highlight any issues can be corrected. By the way, you'll note that it's important to get the entire practice on board when it comes to your...

Reputation Marketing.

Another thing you want included is a daily review alerts system. When a negative review is posted, you want to know. We've found that it's not so much that a negative review is posted, but how you respond to it. And how quickly. We recommend developing a response within twenty-four hours and posting the response to the appropriate review website.

Most prospective patients understand there are always two sides to a story.

What really looks bad is a negative review with no response. That shows a lack of caring or concern on your part.

Managing your reputation isn't just about monitoring or reporting. It's about continuing to grow your reviews. Your prospective patients don't want to see reviews that are six months, a year, even eighteen months old. They want to see up-to-date reviews to know that you are continually giving great service in the marketplace.

You have to keep on posting reviews and understand that the individual can't do it. Each practice needs a system and a process that overrides those review site filters and algorithms. If no system is in place, posted reviews will be deleted the next day.

Step 4: Create Your Culture

Here's our premise:

You're only one patient away from a bad reputation.

We believe you expect your staff to give first-class service to every single one of your patients, right? Do you have a plan to inspire your staff to give first-class service to those patients and get raving reviews?

Our ultimate goal is to build a **Reputation Marketing** culture within your practice so all of your staff members are "on the same page." Each team member in your practice, especially those that interact with patients, completely needs to understand the positive or negative effect he or she can have with a patient. We have dozens of examples of a team member saying something, maybe inadvertently, to a patient that resulted in a negative review being posted within minutes of the patient leaving the office.

So what's your plan? How are you going to, without taking a lot of time on your end, train your staff? You could create a series of short training videos each of your staff can view that outlines their importance in building and maintaining your **5 Star** local online Reputation.

As an option for our members, we've built an education training center for each staff member that they access, understand and learn what **Reputation Marketing** is and, more importantly, the way that they actually treat the patient today is the reason that you are going to get a new patient tomorrow.

Remember, **you're always one patient away from getting a bad reputation online** and your entire staff needs to know it. Therefore, we are able to ensure that your entire team understands by developing a personalized reputation training center for them.

Whether you develop it yourself or have someone like us do it for you, you want to grow and change your culture to make a difference.

Putting It All Together

As we've shown in these two chapters, your knowledge of the power of *Public Referrals©* can give you a significant competitive advantage in your local marketplace.

However, as a very successful friend once told me, "To know and not to do is not to know."

Knowledge is one thing. Application is another.

We've laid out a four-step process so that you can use your knowledge to create, maintain and sustain your unique competitive advantage.

All you have to do is execute.

In summary, because you are a dentist that provides great service in your local marketplace, by building, marketing and managing your **5 Star** reputation to create a culture within your practice, you will have new patients knocking down your door. You will have taken **Reputation Marketing** to a completely new level.

About The Author...

Jon Keel *has developed a local and national reputation as a local business online presence and reputation marketing expert, having been actively involved in this arena since 2008. His most recent company, 5 Star Strategic Results, LLC, which he co-founded in 2013, creates 5 star online reputations and then markets those reputations for several hundred local businesses across the U.S.*

He co-developed the Xavier University MBA E-Business program, where he taught Online Marketing and E-Commerce for over three years.

He frequently speaks to local, regional, and national audiences. He has written numerous articles and has appeared on several TV news and talk programs.

He co-developed the first pay-per-click search engine bid management software in 2000 and wrote the first book on pay-per-click search engines, "Instant Web Site Traffic" (August, 2001). He also contributed to the best-selling book, "Success Secrets of the Online Marketing Superstars," published in 2005. His most recent book, "Secrets of Peak Performers," which he co-authored with Dan Kennedy, Bill Glazer, and Lee Milteer, was published in April, 2009.

Jon moved to Cincinnati in 1971 as an environmental engineer with the Procter and Gamble Company. He left P&G in 1973 to work for The Henry P. Thompson Company, over a 22-year period becoming the owner and President/CEO, before selling his interest in 1995. He received an MBA from Xavier University in 1987

Chapter 16

Applying Your Powers of Social Proof

By **Ron Sheetz**

"You're not paid for what you know; you're paid for who you are and what you can do."

~Napoleon Hill
(Author of the Best-Selling
Business Book, "Think and Grow Rich")

"Last week, I attended my dentist's funeral." My friend Stephan, and a fellow mastermind member, shared this with me recently, knowing that I work with dentists. Stephen told me that he'd gone to high school with his dentist and, as far as he knew, he and his practice were doing well. Not until attending the funeral did Stephan discover that his high school pal had been struggling to keep his practice afloat financially. Stephan told me that he was a good man, a great dentist and civic leader in the community. It came as a shock to him when this pillar of society felt the only way out was to take his own life.

I know this is a grim way to start this chapter, however, it's a growing statistic among dentists. In addition, the state of dentistry is changing; if you don't think so, read Jerry Jones' report of the same title. It conveys a very true picture of where dentistry is heading for the solo-practitioner.

Of the GPs I have as private clients, I see vast similarities in them. They all started a practice to serve their patients, to be the best dentist they could be, and to provide a good life for their families. I've seen a common core principle that every successful dentist understands and leverages in their practice. It's the primary thing most patients are looking for in their dentist(at least as told to me by the hundreds of dental patients I've interviewed over the years) and it's the foundation of the marketing tool I'll reveal in this chapter. No dentist establishes this one thing early enough in the relationship with his or her patients. It's something that develops naturally between the dentist and patient, though it can be accelerated to the point of eliminating fee resistance when it's established properly. I'll share actual case examples later in the chapter from patients who I've interviewed.

"No one cares what you know until they know how much you care."

Author Unknown

I love quotes because I think they encapsulate the essence of key things in life. First, who am I and why should you listen to what I'm about to share with you? I'm not a dentist so how could I know anything about marketing a dental practice? You'd be right, I don't know anything about marketing a dental practice but I do know how to market people because it's how I've grown my business. I'll let you in on a little secret. I don't spend one dime on traditional marketing, yet I have some of the country's most influential

Dr. ManbirPannu
North Royalton Dentist

entrepreneurs as private clients; business people from different industries, including dentistry. People like Jerry Jones, Dr. James McAnally, Dr. Tom Orent, Dr. Chris Griffin and Dan Kennedy (a leading marketing strategist to dentists for the past thirty years), not to mention dozens of solo-dentists just like you, who you'll meet in the following paragraphs.

My journey in helping dentists started with my own family dentist, Dr. Manbir Pannu, in North Royalton, Ohio. Manbir is retired from the US Army and is a Lieutenant Colonel in the US Army Reserves. She served troops during Operation Iraqi Freedom. She's a great person, a fabulous GP and passionate about her practice and patients (sound familiar?). With two operatories, running the practice, doing all the dentistry herself, including cleanings, she struggled to grow her practice. She had advocate patients (like me), a solid practice and state-of-the-art equipment, but struggled to expand it. I offered to help and the one strategy (actually two, but interpreted by patients as one) that I'll share with you here brought more new patients in one month than any month in her practice history. Don't misunderstand me; I know nothing about the science behind dentistry, however, I know what patients want and I know how to give it to them in the marketing message.

Dr. Pannu serving US troops during Operation Iraqi Freedom

I'll tip my hat a bit here. Dr. Pannu had all the right elements to share her story with patients, but she wasn't using it in her marketing, not at all. In her marketing, she was selling teeth whitening, free exams, free consultations and discounts...like so many other dentists advertising to the same group of patients.

What elements did she possess, but wasn't using? Two, actually. Her personal story and letting advocate patients share their stories about being a patient in her practice. Initially, I created a brief 'Meet the Doctor' video for her website along with audio interviews with patients. You can see the video on her website. The key to connecting with prospective patients was telling her story and patient testimonials. I don't have enough space in this chapter to discuss the true power behind story telling in marketing and it won't be my focus here, but if you've followed Jerry Jones long enough, and have studied his style of marketing, you already understand. As for patient testimonials, that's my specialty and most dentists I meet and talk with understand that patient testimonials are valuable to have in their marketing, yet most struggle to get them. Out of those that do have them, most aren't squeezing every ounce of equity they could out of them.

You too, may be a dentist who's tried to implement a system for getting testimonials from patients, yet struggled to make it work. By the time you're done reading this chapter, you'll understand not only how to get a testimonial but what a great one looks and sounds like. I'll reveal the techniques and strategies I've developed – the ones my private clients hire me to implement for them.

What are patient testimonials?

I was taught never to assume that someone knows something because I myself know it. So, if you know what a testimonial is, bear with me. Simply put, a patient testimonial is social proof. It's another person speaking about their experience with you, your practice or your team and the results they gained from that relationship with you. You'll notice I wrote, "Their experience with you..." For the patient, it's all about the experience.

As I'm writing this, 74% of the US population fears the dentist, or fears going to the dentist. This is a huge obstacle for you in attracting new patients, let alone getting them to accept the cases you present to them. My client Dr. Robert Matiasevich, in Santa Cruz, California sums up marketing his practice like this, *"The biggest challenge I face in marketing my practice, isn't getting the new patient to come into the practice, it's getting them to pick up the phone and call the practice."*

Dr. Bob Matiasevich
Santa Cruz Family
Dentistry

Robert Collier, a successful marketer and author of *The Robert Collier Letter Book* (published in 1937) wrote that the quickest way to connect with a prospect, in your case prospective patients, is to enter the conversation already going on in their mind. What are the conversations they're having with themselves, their spouse, friends or coworkers when they're looking for a dentist? Seventy-four percent of them don't want to go to a dentist to start with and they have an even bigger problem changing dentists even when their experience with the existing dentist isn't good.

Dr. David Pearce
Baldwinsville Gentle
Dentistry

The idea of changing dentists to look for another is more painful than enduring poor care from their present one.

Picture that new patient who does overcome the fear and calls your practice. As they stand outside the door of your practice for the first time, they unconsciously (or consciously) ask themselves, how will my experience with this dentist be any different from my past dental experiences? In a moment, you'll meet Shannon Wright, who asked herself that very question before she found her dentist, Dr. David Pearce (Baldwinsville Gentle Dentistry, Baldwinsville, New York) and one of my clients.

Here's a transcription from an actual dental patient. Angela's comment clearly illustrates both what you're fighting as a dentist in attracting new patients and the conversation going on in the minds of people.

Angela Stoutenger
Patient

"I had received flyers in the mail from this practice. I just stuck it into my pile and thought maybe when I go to the dentist I'll think about going to them, then, I thought, you know it's really time, I really need to go to the dentist. I was really torn because another coworker was going to a different dentist in Baldwinsville and she had just started going to him and she had been having a good experience so I was really was torn between the two but, I don't know, there was something about Dr. Pearce, I don't even remember if it was something about what they said and, I don't know, I just thought to myself, this is the dentist for me."

You see a patient testimonial can enter the conversation your prospective patients are having with themselves. In direct selling, those conversations are called obstacles or objections. They're the things that keep a patient from picking up the phone and calling the practice. They're also what prevent the patient from accepting your case presentation because, unless we address and answer these objections, it's a struggle to convince a patient that the case you present, no matter the fee, is the right one for them. It comes down to trust. As a dentist, you're in the trust business. To break the fee resistance barrier with patients completely, they have to trust you.

Your patients are trying to figure out nine things about you and trust will only be established when the patient is fully satisfied.

When you analyze the patients that you have now, those that accept your diagnosis and plans with little or no hesitation, you will find that they've already satisfied these nine concerns about you. Once these nine concerns are addressed and satisfied, the patient will see you as a trusted dental advisor rather than a dentist peddling his or her services.

The Nine Things They Are Trying to Figure Out About You

1. Authenticity - Are you real? Or is the marketing hype?
2. Believability - Are you telling the truth?
3. Credibility - Are you knowledgeable and competent?

4. Feasibility of the relationship - Are you appropriate for them? Can they see themselves being comfortable with you?
5. Customized solutions - Are you listening to them or are they just a number in the practice?
6. Safety/Security - Are you reliable and can you be relied upon?
7. Comfort - Do they understand enough about what you can do for them
8. Superiority - Are they making the best choice versus other choices available?
9. Value - Are they paying a 'fair' fee?

* (The '9 Things' are borrowed from Dan Kennedy and his Trust-Based Marketing event, upon which I produced the recorded content)

I won't go into detail on each of these, because they're self-explanatory. I provide this merely for your understanding that prospective patients are judging you against these nine fundamental criteria. As a consumer of products or services yourself, you're making these same determinations, consciously or unconsciously.

Their importance increases equally as the investment for a product or service increases.

Patient testimonials and the sharing of their experiences with you will significantly accelerate a new patient to draw a positive conclusion on these fundamentals.

What others say about you is a thousand times more effective, impactful and influential than what you would say on your own behalf. Napoleon Hill wrote, *"They won't hear you until they know you."* They won't trust you until they've figured out these nine things about you and when they do, they'll feel they know you; when they know you, they'll hear you. They'll hear your case presentation from an open, non-adversarial position.

Without first having created and established trust, your case presentation will be heard through defensive guard. The patient will have their guard up. Think of a professional boxer who holds fists in front of his face to protect himself from the opponent's jabs and punches.

It's unavoidable, but every selling situation, including case presentations, creates an adversarial situation. Your patient in the role of the opponent, with hands rose to their face to protect themselves from jabs and punches is on guard for the 'price' of the dental case.

Remember, most patients have had poor experiences with well-intentioned, but ignorant dentists; their words not mine. There are two things I hear consistently from patients I interview: 1- they felt treated only as a number on a medical chartand2- they felt the doctor recommended dental work only to 'up the bill!' You're facing these obstacles. Whether they tell you or not, you must recognize it. Testimonials are a powerful tool to dispel these beliefs and cut through past dental 'baggage.'

Using patient testimonials allows prospective patients to read about others' experiences. It gives your prospective patient a model against which to decide if you are right for them (#4 from the list), are you reliable (#6), have you heard their concerns and addressed it in your dental plan (#5) and is the value greater than the fee paid in exchange for the plan (#9)?

Now, let's consider your position on testimonials. There are three types of people when it comes to the use of testimonials in advertising and marketing.

1. The first type of person doesn't recognize testimonials when they read, hear or see them.
2. The second type recognizes testimonials in advertising and marketing, however, they don't know how they could be applied in their own advertising or marketing.
3. And the third recognizes the value of testimonials, has them and is applying them in their advertising and marketing, but not to their fullest extent.

Later in this chapter, I'll show you thirty-three different ways you can apply a single video testimonial in advertising and marketing, and four ways it can affect your case acceptance numbers almost immediately.

Until now, I've spoken only of patient testimonials and only here have I mentioned video testimonials. I've done that strategically. When I say "patient testimonials," most dentists think of written or spoken testimonials, yet when I mention the idea of actually getting a patient to give a testimonial on video, I'm often told, "We've tried to get them from patients, but haven't been successful at it. "It's not that they or you can't get them; you just haven't had the right tools, until now.

Types of Patient Video Testimonials

There are two types of patient video testimonials: The delivered testimonial and the interview testimonial.

#1 - *The Delivered Testimonial*

The delivered testimonial is the most common. A delivered testimonial is one where the patient stands before the video camera and talks extemporaneously. Without advanced coaching or guidance, they often rattle off the first things that come to their mind. These are often well-intentioned comments, but they are void of any long-term marketable content. These testimonials typical reflect adoration for the doctor and/or staff. Here are transcripts from actual patient video testimonials captured by Dr. David Pearce's team prior to me teaching them how to capture powerful patient testimonials.

You can see they speak highly of the doctor and practice; however, these are what I call 'feel-good' testimonials. There are three major components missing from these examples: the patient's backstory, what the catalyst for treatment was and their results. A patient's backstory is a powerful point of connection for prospective patients and positive results are what every patient is interested in.

You can tell from these examples they like the practice, but as a viewer, I don't know what led them to this doctor (backstory), what he or she did for them and what the outcome was (results). These testimonials are too general. They'll leave a viewer (your prospective patient) thinking, "That's nice, but it doesn't apply to me because my case is different."

Without connecting your prospective patient to your existing patients (through experiences) the testimony has no validity and therefore just a bunch of hot air.

"I came to this dental office today on an emergency basis and they got me in immediately. This is the friendliest dental office I've ever been in the years I've been alive."

"This is my first visit to Dr. Pearce Gentle Dentistry. The first experience was great. I felt very relaxed and very well taken care of and it was a pleasant experience."

"What I enjoyed about my first appointment was that the staff was very friendly, they answered all of my questions. They talked to me step by step through the process of what they were going to do and the dentist came in and rather than just checking my teeth and leaving he made sure he talked to me for a few minutes and addressed all of my issues and concerns that I had."

"Every time I come into Dr. Pearce's office the staff is great, they're friendly, the service is good and I enjoy coming back."

People connect with other people because of shared stories or experiences. When I interview a patient, I'm always probing for their stories; what they went through that brought them to where they are today. Therein lies connection with other patients for your practice. If a prospective patient doesn't connect with the story, it's just rhetoric, and it's not effective marketing for you.

Understanding the pain behind your patient's journey helps a prospective patient appreciate the results the testifying patient received. I call this "doctor benefit by proxy. "The prospective patient's mindset is, "that patient is like me and Dr. X was able to help him or her, so Doctor X can help me."

Having said that, not all delivered testimonials are bad or useless. There are people who can nail it. They can give a very content-rich delivered testimonial. I've found these types of people to be very introspective. They're both emotionally and intellectually motivated. However, they're rare.

I've reviewed thousands of delivered testimonials and when you hear them one after another, they all tend to say the same. This isn't the fault of the patient; they don't know what to say.

With a little guidance about what to say, you can capture some great delivered testimonials. The guidance you can provide them can be borrowed from the interview testimonial, which I'll cover next.

Simply borrow the format I'll show you and give it to them as bullet points to follow when they give their testimonial. The challenge I find with this is that most people are not capable of articulating themselves well. What ends up happening is they become so focused on trying to hit all the points you've asked them to that they stammer and their delivery becomes a distraction from the content, which equates to a loss of credibility.

#2 - *The Interview Testimonial*

The second type of testimonial is one captured by interviewing a patient rather than letting them speak impromptu. Think of film or TV documentaries; they're in depth case studies on their subject. I developed my method of interviewing patients and creating detailed dental practice documentaries from studying hundreds and hundreds of feature film documentaries. It took me a long time to convince my accountant that the movie DVDs I bought were a business expense and should be classified under continued education (I love the films too, but that's a residual benefit).

My client Dan Kennedy is the most highly paid and sought after direct response copywriter in the world; so I think he knows a thing or two about influencing people through writing. In fact, he calls what he does, "salesmanship in print." That's what you need to do, whether you like it or not, is to influence people, sell them on your approach to their dental care as being the best approach for them (that goes back to the 9 fundamentals model, #5 – customized solutions).

To simplify the model, Mr. Kennedy follows a problem, agitate, solution model in much of his writing. Pay attention here, you'll begin to see the similarities develop with what I wrote earlier.

Presenting the backstory or problem first provides the point of connection and it's important to connect with prospective patients early; this is an engagement technique.

Next, agitating the problem with their symptoms elevates the pain. It's like applying salt in an open wound.

Finally, the solution obtained by following the same action the subject in the story did; your existing patient. This is a very effective selling model to follow.

Here's the model that I adapted from it and use for patient testimonials.

- Pain
- Turning point
- Solution

What is the patient's pain? It could be physical tooth pain or the life-long embarrassment of a crooked smile that they hide behind their hand every time they smile.

What was the turning point? What was the catalyst that motivated them to seek out a dentist to fix the problem? There's always one major thing. It's the 'thing' that finally clicked for them to take action!

Seventy-four percent of the US population fears the dentist. I've lost count of how many patients I've interviewed that told me of the five, ten, thirty or forty-five-year hiatus they took from seeing a dentist. I also hear from patients how they endured well intentioned, but poor, dental care because it was easier than finding a new dentist – not to mention their fear of entering a worse dental care situation than they were in already.

Finally, what's the solution? For my private dental clients, the solution is always them and their practice. Through compelling patient interview testimonials, a prospective patient clearly sees the best solution, the only real solution, is you! I use this model. These are the components of a great testimonial.

Here's transcript from another patient interview and captured on video for a private client. You will clearly be able to identify the pain, turning point and solution model within this testimonial.

Shannan Wright
Patient

"I'm terrified of the dentist, terrified. Like by terrified I mean cold sweet breaking out and running down my face. It started way back when I was a little girl, I mean, I had a dentist pull a tooth, an impacted tooth. I was ten, and he said that I was being a baby. But he hadn't given me enough Novocain, and the next thing that I remember is kicking him and running out and blood was running down my face and my mother was horrified. Maybe I just picked the wrong dentist and I'm glad that I finally picked one that's a winner. I was finally forced to find a dentist when the Anbesoland Tylenol would no longer make the pain go away from my tooth that was abscessed. I cannot place a value on anything that Dr. Pearce has done with my dental work; I can't. It really has changed my life. I smile more, I laugh more, I take more pictures, you know like family pictures. I don't sit in the corner anymore. I talk to people. When you have really bad teeth you try to

*cover them and hide them. You become a master
and an expert at it. I don't have to do that
anymore; you know, I mean it's, now, I literally
have <u>the</u> perfect smile, <u>the</u> perfect smile for me. Dr.
Pearce was everything I needed him to be."*

But what questions do you ask a patient?

The questions are subjective to your practice. If I
were working with you to develop a powerful patient
video testimonial library or documentary film about
your practice, I'd ask you about what obstacles or
objections you encounter during case presentations;
those that prevent patients from moving forward with
the dental plans you present. Simply formulate
questions that address those objections and then ask
your existing patients the right questions that lead
them to answers that will overcome those objections.

How do you get patient testimonials?

When I speak before groups of dentists, I ask for
a show of hands of how many are actually getting video
testimonials. Usually it's a third of the room—that's not
bad. Then I ask how many find it a struggle to get
them; or, alternatively, dentists who struggle with their
teams to get them? Here's why.

I'll first approach it from your team's
perspective. Your team is uncomfortable asking for
video testimonials. They wouldn't be comfortable going
on camera if asked; therefore, they're uncomfortable
asking others to do it.

They also feel awkward asking. These are two different things. Hygienist Donna Collins shared with me during an interview once, "You know, the doctor wants us to get video testimonies, but I just feel icky asking." Those were her exact words. "I feel icky." Questioning her further, it was because she thought that asking her patients to go on video was outside the scope of the relationship she'd developed with her patients.

When I showed her how to ask, it completely changed her mindset and comfort level. She no longer felt icky asking. The problem was that she had stinking thinking and she was asking the wrong way.

Additionally, your team may not understand the real value of testimonials and what they mean for the practice. Some people are just technologically challenged. They just don't like the technology.

From the patient perspective, they're shy; they don't like cameras. They don't like the way they look or sound on camera. They also don't know what to say. I described it earlier with the delivered testimonials. These testimonials often contain verbal vomit. No one likes being put on the spot.

Without properly preparing a patient before asking them to give you a video testimonial would constitute putting them on the spot. Their instinctive response will be fight or flight. They'll give you all kinds of reasons why they can't do it or they'll just say no. Either way you haven't gotten a video testimonial and asking patients incorrectly could potentially tarnish your relationship with that patient.

So, when do you ask for a video testimonial (or any testimonial for that matter)? You ask when the patient's in what I call the 'glow' state.

You must be on the lookout for testimonial triggers. They're spontaneous words, feelings or expressions from the patient that indicate they're in the 'glow.' The glow is when they're feeling good about you and what you've done for them and they're telling you or someone else about it.

For example, this may be when the patient is checking out at the reception desk and they're telling your receptionist about how glad they are they found you, or how they couldn't be happier with the work you've done, or how much they love your hygienist.

When you hear these types of statements, you know it's the appropriate time to ask. The key is *how* you ask. Remember I said no one likes being put on the spot? Even when you hear them waxing enthusiasm over you, if you were to ask them, "Can you give me a video testimonial?" it still would be abrupt.

Here's how you ask. This is the script I've developed, tested and taught countless dental practices.

Let's imagine your patient says one of the following things to the receptionist.

"You guys are miracle workers."
"I didn't think it was possible to have the smile I've always dreamed of."

"I never liked coming to the dentist, but you're different."

These are testimonial triggers. If I were in your office, had a video camera and heard a patient utter these words, I'd be on them like a bee on honey. And here's what I'd say:

"Thank you Mrs. Jones, I hear that a lot and I really appreciate you sharing that with me. Would you mind if I ask a favor of you? Would you mind if I shared your thoughts about us with others just like you? There many people who are afraid of the dentist and, as you stated, we're not scary. If I can share your experience with us, with others, hopefully we can help more people just like you. Because we'd love to have more patients just like you. Would it be ok if I did that?"

This is the set up. This conversation prepares them for what you'll ask next. You'll notice I haven't said anything about getting a testimonial or asking her to get in front of a camera. There's a lot of psychology at work in this script. First, I expressed appreciation for her comments (gratitude is important) and I asked three questions that will elicit a yes response every time. This is called the rule of three. When I can get three successive yesses from the patient, I've worked them into an agreement pattern. Once they're in an agreement pattern, they're likely to say yes to the next thing I ask, which is going to be giving me a video testimonial. Here's the tie-down question:

"Great, I'd like to capture your thoughts on my little pocket camera so others can hear it directly from you.

I couldn't do justice to how well you said it and they probably wouldn't believe me. You won't have to remember what you said; I'll just ask you a couple of questions to help you repeat what you said. Would that be ok? It would be a big help to us."

Once again, there's psychology behind this tie down question. The key is in the language I use and its structure. You'll notice I never use the word video or record. Instead, I say capture and little pocket camera. The language is critical; it minimizes the patient's fear.

Because of the way I structure the question, in their mind, they're not recording a video or giving a testimonial, they're sharing their thoughts, which they just did – so they're simply going to be repeating themselves and not having to figure out what to say. At the end I ask, *"Would that be ok?"* They could say no, but I don't pause and I ensure they won't say no by applying a little motherly guilt: *"It would be a big help to us."* It works because I've tested it repeatedly with different approaches and this is the best one – tried and true. In addition, I come from an Italian family and the hierarchy of Italian families rule through guilt.

I'm also offering them the opportunity to help someone else. There's a reciprocal component working here. You have helped them and now they can return the favor to you. By nature, people are willing to help. If you approached an entrance door with your hands full and couldn't open the door, it's likely a nearby person would help by opening the door for you.

This all may sound a bit uncomfortable and it is at first, but it works! And, yes, it takes a little more effort than just asking, "Would you give me a video testimonial." The results, however, are drastically better. Anything worth doing is worth doing well. Anything worth doing well isn't likely to be easy. If it were easy, everyone would be doing it.

Learn this simple script, implement it and I guarantee you'll capture patient video testimonials that are more valuable and marketable than you've ever gotten before.

How to leverage your video social proof in your practice

You can use the techniques and strategies I've shared with you here to capture written testimonials, but you're doing yourself a disservice by not pursuing video testimonials.

There are several advantages of having video testimonials over just a written testimonial. Video is so effective because it is the closest form of communication to an in-person conversation.

There's tremendous power in being able to see a person's body language and hear the authenticity of emotion in a person's voice. A UCLA professor conducted a study on effective communication and found that 55% of the communication between people occurred in body language, gestures and facial expressions, while 37% of the communication takes place in how a person says what they say in their voice and tonality, and only 8% of communication is in the actual words.

In having only written testimonial, you're missing 92% of the true power of communicating with prospective patients.

Another effective opportunity with video testimonials is that it can be applied in your marketing and advertising in three different mediums: video, audio and print.

A video testimonial consists of video, audio and words. You can insert testimonials in video form on your website or play them on the big screen TV in your patient waiting area.

You can extract the audio from the video and use an excerpt in a radio commercial or on your website. Have the audio from the video transcribed and use nuggets from it in print advertising.

You can also lift a still frame captured from the video in picture form and apply it with the text version of the testimonial. All that from one video testimonial.

But wait, there's more. I've identified thirty-three different ways a single video testimonial can be applied to your marketing and advertising. Bear in mind, not all thirty-three ways may be applicable to you. It depends largely on what media you're using to promote your practice. In any event, here's the list broken down by the three mediums: video, audio and print.

Applied in video/audio form:
1. As a video on your website
2. On a branded YouTube channel

3. Facebook posts
4. Compilation video DVD to ride along with a physical proposal
5. Video playback in the lobby where your clients/patients will see it
6. Video bytes in television commercials
7. Video attachment (physical or electronic) submitted along with a media release
8. Part of an automated follow up sequence to prospective patients (physically or electronically)
9. Automated follow up "stick" material to patients (physical or electronically)
10. Playback during a live presentation
11. Playback during a teleconference or webinar
12. Add to your smart phone or tablet for access during spontaneous presentations
13. Video blog posts
14. Testimonial-based info-documentary about your business (long-format video marketing – positioning tool to leverage authority, expert, celebrity)

Applied in audio form only:

15. Sound bites as part of telephone on-hold message
16. Inserted into radio commercials
17. Part of a pod-cast
18. Inserted into voice broadcasts
19. Audio playback during live presentations
20. Compilation audio CD to ride along with a take home materials
21. Website
22. Teleseminar

Applied transcribed in text form:

23. Billboard advertising
24. Signage
25. Websites
26. Faxes
27. Written proposals (physical or electronic)
28. Text messages (mobile marketing)
29. Live presentations
30. On paperwork (don't exclude patient testimonials from the forms patients are required to fill out – A.B.M. – Always Be Marketing)
31. Brochures
32. List of services
33. Newspaper/print advertising mediums

Earlier, I told you that I don't spend a dime on traditional marketing and advertising. The bulk of my marketing is done through referrals and testimonial marketing. I can tell you from experience in having interviewed so many dental patients and dentists, that a majority of your practice's new patients are likely coming from referrals and word of mouth marketing.

However, referrals are the most undeveloped and systematized marketing avenue in many practices. When a patient tells me they've referred others to their dentist, I always ask if they know if that person ever followed through to contact the practice or became a patient. The typical response is, "I don't know," hence the absence of a system to generate and track referred patients.

The Fastest Path to Case Acceptance (the cash)

You face two major challenges from a business perspective, in getting new patients to the practice and getting those patients to accept the cases presented.

Next, I'll show you how to apply video testimonial marketing into your new patient process or funnel. This is a simplification of the process a new patient experiences on their initial visit to your practice. Yours may vary, though the premise is the same. Focus on the principles, not necessarily the process.

A new patient can come to your practice through various sources: referrals, word of mouth, television, radio, display ads, direct mail, newsletters, billboards, etc. Regardless of how the patient finds you, video testimonials can elevate and differentiate your position, in the prospective patient's mind, over competing dentists in your area.

First, understand that seeing a dentist is not high on the list of things that people love to do.

Remember Dr. Matiasevich's statement earlier? *"My biggest marketing challenge is not to get the patient in for an appointment; it's getting them to pick up the phone and call to make an appointment."* It's becoming more difficult to motivate patients to call your practice. There now are big corporate practices offering cheap dentistry, selling their services mostly on low prices, ultimately devaluing and commoditizing dentistry.

Traditional methods of getting patients are becoming obsolete and ineffective. I see little dental advertising that includes patient testimonials, let alone any full-blown testimonial marketing; marketing made up entirely of testimonials.

Traditional marketing relies on promoting an offer or opportunity such as an introductory exam or cleaning. Most dental marketing is geared at promoting the deliverable rather than promoting the results, let alone the doctor.

During our interview together, Dr. Zan Beaver of First Coast Family Dental, shared with me that in measuring traffic to his website, he found that people spent X% more time at the meet the doctor and meet the staff pages. Not only are they the most visited pages, they're also the pages people stay engaged with the longest. Patients tell me that when visiting a doctor's website they like to see a picture of the doctor and learn more about him or her.

Most decide if they like the doctor based on his or her picture and story. Imagine how much more powerful this would be if your site included your picture and a short "Meet the Doctor" video along with patient testimonials, adding credibility to your claims (marketing).

For your patients, their satisfaction with you and your practice depends on two critical factors: Your skills as a dentist and your chairside manner. They need to know, like and trust you.

You can have the best skills in the world, but if you don't have a great, or even a good, chairside manner, you're not going to develop long-term patients.

There are only two ways a patient can determine whether they like you and can trust you: Through a referral (proxy) or actually meeting you.

For the patient, it's all about the experience.

All too often, their true experience with you doesn't begin until they come into the practice. Sure, they can talk to your receptionist on the phone and they can check out your website, but the true measure is when they step through your door and experience it for themselves. Only then will they really know what it's like to be a patient in your practice.

Video testimonials are a pivotal component in positioning you and your practice in the mind of the patient and it can have a significant effect on whether a patient follows through with a visit.

More importantly, it will affect whether the patient proceeds with the case you present and at the fee you present. Here's a general look at the average new patient practice funnel.

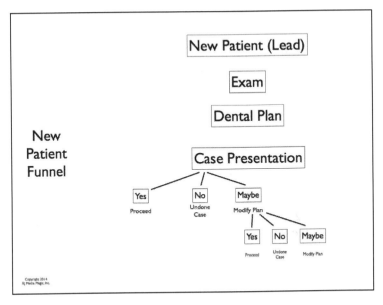

A typical dental practice new patient funnel

The patient enters the practice and gets an initial exam. From the exam, you identify opportunities for dental work.

I see dentists who create long-term strategies of the plan being implemented over a period and those that offer good-better-best alternative plans from which the patient can choose.

In either event, once the plan is developed, the case is presented. In direct selling, we call this the sales conversation. It's the dreaded uncomfortable part for doctor and patient in this newly forming relationship... it's where you get to talk price.

I find few doctors like presenting the price and even fewer patients like hearing it, but it's an inevitable part of the relationship and the key word here is *relationship*. You want to establish a relationship with your patient, and they with you, but too often money gets in the way.

Why? If you're getting sticker shock when you present the fees for a case, it's because you haven't created enough value to offset the fee. Fee resistance is when the fee is higher than the value the patient receives in exchange for the fee.

Recently, I interviewed Jeff Wiebe, a patient of Dr. Steve Garrett's Hillsborough Family Dentistry in Hillsborough, North Carolina. He told me that Dr. Garrett recommended that he needed a bridge that would cost $3,800.

Jeff Wiebe, Patient

I asked Jeff if he'd sought a second opinion or quote on the diagnosis? He told me no and when I asked why not his reply was, "He's my dentist and I trust him."

This is where you want to be with every patient in every case presentation. The value of what the patient receives has to outweigh the fee the patient will invest in the dentistry. When achieved, this will help you eliminate fee resistance. How do you accomplish this? Start the patient's experience with you sooner in the relationship.

The following model illustrates where you can apply video testimonials to accomplish this. You'll see that I'm working on developing the value of their relationship with you sooner and more frequently than typical.

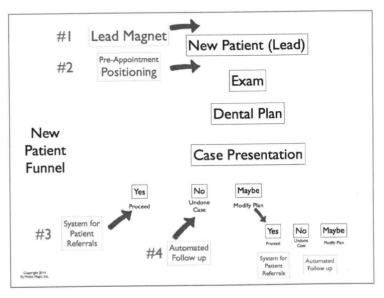

Patient Video Testimonials interjected into the new patient funnel

1st A DVD of your patient video testimonials can be used as a piece that prospective patients can request. This is called a lead magnet. The concept is that rather than attract patients through traditional offers (free exams, free x-rays, etc.), you advertise to send patients a DVD offering them the opportunity to experience what it's like to be your patient.

Prospective patients call the practice or go online to request the DVD in exchange for sharing their mailing address with you, hence the capture of a lead.

The travel industry has employed this marketing strategy for many years. Understand that it does delay the patient actually contacting your practice to schedule an appointment, but there is great benefit in delaying the appointment. You're working on developing the relationship before you start selling dentistry.

Unlike traditional advertising, it sends a different message to prospective patients. Whereas traditional advertising and offers communicate that a case presentation (sales pitch for dentistry) will likely ensue, offering a DVD and giving the prospective patient the chance to check you out sends an entirely different message.

I've gained many clients through this method of marketing. It's both delaying the sale and a bit of take away selling.

Traditional advertising telegraphs that you want a patient's business; it communicates that you're going to sell something, just like every other dentist.

Offering them information about you, which they're going to investigate anyway, actually speeds your ability to build rapport with them. This form of advertising communicates, *"We're here and we're in no hurry to sell you. Check us out and decide for yourself if we're right for you. If we are, we'd love to see you, if we're not, no harm, no foul."* It's a much more natural and relaxed way of presenting you and your practice. Patients are also highly susceptible to this approach to marketing.

This is very similar to referral marketing. When an existing, advocate patient refers someone to you, the new patient is in a more advanced stage in their buying process than the patient who comes to you through traditional advertising. We call that the difference between a warm and cold lead.

The new patient's experience should begin long before they call or visit your practice. No one likes to be 'sold,' but everyone loves to buy something they seek. A DVD of testimonials or a documentary film about your practice offers prospective patients the opportunity to see and hear what it's like to be a patient in your practice before they ever have to commit to picking up the phone and scheduling that first appointment.

2ⁿᵈ When a patient comes to the practice through traditional marketing or advertising, they can be mailed your DVD of patient testimonials before their first appointment (when time allows – but you can control this).

Don't wait for the patient to visit you to allow the patient experience to begin, as most every other practice does. You should get a jump on it. Don't allow the patient experience to just happen; control it. How much more receptive do you think a patient would be to your case presentation and fee if they enter the practice pre-qualified to expect a higher level of dentistry and care than they would from any other practice?

Two things will happen: you'll elevate the quality of the patients entering the practice and you'll attract more of your ideal patients. You'll also repel a certain percentage of prospective patients.

This isn't a bad thing. Those patients, who watch your testimonial DVD or practice documentary film and find you're not the type of dentist they're comfortable with will not come to your practice. Sending this type of information, you'll have invested only a few dollars for the DVD and shipping and saved the valuable time you would have wasted on an exam, time to develop and present a plan only to have them say no, not to mention the cost and time for your staff to process the patient and paperwork.

3rd For patients who have the propensity to refer you, a patient testimonial DVD or documentary film can create the systematized referral process I spoke of earlier.

A customized dental practice documentary film strategically incorporating filmed patient interview testimonials

One-thousand DVDs ready for mailing to patients of the newly acquired practice

The traditional referral tool I see practices using is a business card. They're cheap and easy to hand out. Patients can be instructed to give them away to friends, family members or coworkers and puts your contact information in their hands, but what ultimately happens to those business cards?

Business cards are small and easily lost or forgotten. Instead, provide patients with a properly packaged testimonial DVD they can hand out.

This is an example of the type of documentary films I produce for private clients. Depending on the quantity, these can be reproduced for a little more than a dollar and they have a greater perceived value than a business card. In addition, they're harder for patients to throw away or lose and, unlike a business card, your DVD can actually tell your story and is an excellent way to start the relationship with a prospective patient and to position you differently from other dentists. Perception is reality.

Additionally, your patient, the person referring you and passing on the DVD, doesn't have to be a great salesperson. All they need to do is give away the DVDs for you. I provide my clients with a very simple one-liner they can teach their patients to say when giving away the DVDs. Including some type of offer or bounce-back inside the DVD that allows you to track referral activity.

Not too long after completing the documentary film about their practice, one of my clients purchased a second practice. We leveraged the film a step further by sending patients in the acquired practice a DVD introducing him or her to their new dentist.

The objective was to minimize patient attrition during the transition, as well as elevate the patient's expectation for the new docs. So far, it's proved very effective. The new practice is already showing growth under the new owners.

4 <u>th</u> What about those patients that don't proceed with a case? What do they do? What do you do? There's money in the follow- up of these abandoned or undone cases.

Too often, I see practices that don't follow up on patients who took the time and effort to come in for an exam, get a dental plan worked up, hear the case presentation and then don't proceed.

With these patients, you've already invested in them through your marketing and advertising dollars and in the time to see them on the initial exam. Why would you want to leave money on the table and abandon them? Those patients that don't proceed with your case are either going to find another doctor, and proceed with their case or, the more likely thing to happen, is they'll do nothing.

These patients still have the need and it's not likely that need is going away any time soon. Why not follow up with them? Not with aggressive marketing, but rather with important information. One of the most renowned sales trainers, Zig Ziglar, used to teach that people who initially say no to an offer they later say yes to don't change their mind about the offer, but rather make a new decision based on new information.

There's no telling why a patient may turn down your case, but they may say yes at a different time. You would never abandon a patient in need. Why would you abandon a prospective patient in need? You'd actually be doing that person a disservice if you did.

Patient video testimonials can be formatted and applied into an automated email follow-up campaign. Depending on how detailed you want to get, the testimonials selected for the campaign can be targeted toward the needs of each patient.

For example, a prospect who comes to you for orthodontics can receive only those patients you've performed orthodontics on, or a prospect who needs implants will hear only from your implant patients, etc. These sequences can be set-up and launched automatically. It can be a set it and forget it campaign that continually works in the background to turn those 'no' prospects into 'yes' patients. Best of all, these types of automated sequences can cost little to no money depending on your existing systems. If you're an Infusionsoft or similar system user, this is a no brainer.

I've just given you four ways to apply patient video testimonials into your new patient funnel for your practice.

Go back and review my list of thirty-three ways to leverage video testimonials in your marketing as a whole, and in a very short time, with little effort and some imagination, you can start interjecting patient testimonials in all your communications.

I'll leave you with this final quote, because I think it's extremely accurate considering everything I've covered here.

Leonard Bernard Shaw wrote, *"The problem with communication is the illusion that it's taken place."* Which is to say, just because you know something to be true, doesn't mean that others will know it as you have.

Never underestimate the power of communicating with your patients and prospective patients with patient video testimonials. With very little effort, time and investment, you can significantly improve the quality and effectiveness of your marketing, advertising and communications to people who are not yet patients in your practice.

There is significantly more I have to say on the subject of patient video testimonials, but am limited here by space. If you would like to discover more on how to use and implement patient video testimonials into your practice go to www.PatientVideoTestimonials.com/dentalsuccess to get my completer report and case study. As a reader of this Dental Success book you'll also receive my guide to the 31 different ways I've identified how you can use a single video testimonial in your practice marketing and advertising. There's nothing to buy, only provide your name and email address and you'll be emailed both the report and guide immediately, electronically.

About The Author...

Ron Sheetz *is the founder of RJ Media Magic, Inc. He has become an expert in the application of television communication with more than three decades of experience. He has private clients in thirty-seven different industries including the dental industry with Dentists as clients across the U.S., Canada, Australia and Taiwan. He's been widely published in several dental specific books and thought leaders' member publications. He's a highly sought after speaker on the subject of use and application of testimonials and relationship marketing. He publishes three different newsletters each month and leads mastermind sessions on the subject. Ron is also a professional magician and certified hypnotherapist. He lives between two homes, primary residence in a suburb of Cleveland, Ohio, and a second in Orlando, Florida, with his wife Anne and two children, Brandon and Olivia.*

Get my complete report and case study on patient video testimonials atwww.PatientVideoTestimonials.com/dentalsuccess. Provide your name and email address and you'll receive the report immediately along with my guide to the31 different ways I've identified how to use a single patient video testimonial in your practice marketing and advertising just for purchasing this book.

www.patientvideotestimonials.com/dentalsuccess

Chapter 17

Implementation

What to do next and the important part of success:

IMPLEMENTATION

This last section deals with what you should do next, if what you've read in this book resonates, makes sense and inspires you to take the next step.

1. The absolute first "must do" is to request the free audio CD mentioned on the front cover of this book.

    There's no "catch," no cost and no obligation. On this CD, you'll get a chance to "meet" my co-authors and myself, as we're interviewed by fellow author, Mr. Ron Sheetz.

Not only will you hear invaluable information on this CD (truthfully, it alone should sell for at least $99), you'll also get a better understanding of what each of us are about, our main points to help you succeed and more. Go to www.DentalSuccessBook.com

2. In addition, without taking the next step, while this book might be informative for you, it will hold little value unless you fight tooth and nail to implement what you've learned.

Without taking action, this book is merely entertainment that you can get that from mindless TV and hours of interweb surfing, neither of which get you closer to your goals of developing your vision and purpose. The only thing that will get you closer is to move in that direction through implementation.

3. Next, I'd recommend you immediately subscribe to my monthly dental business audio series. These "mini-seminars" are audio CDs (or .mp3 downloads) with full transcripts of me interviewing a variety of business experts both IN dentistry and outside our industry. You can learn more at www.DentistryConfidential.net.At the time of this printing, it is only $9.95/month.

If you're a super-implementer and want to take action even faster, there is no question you'll benefit from the tens of thousands of dollars of immediate value you'll find in my Clear Path Society®. Clear Path Society® is a mastermind of successful, like-minded dentists that meet twice yearly, receive a license to my most successful ads for driving hordes of new patients through your doors, along with other successful dental business systems you receive access to as a Member. More information is available at www.ClearPathSociety.com

4. Finally, I have to mention my latest development and contribution to dentistry, Wellness Springs Dental®; dentistry's ONLY true dental office franchise. It's based on my successful non-doctor-owned dental office in Salem, Oregon. If you're interested in teaming up with a cutting-edge group of business professionals to take your dental practice(s) to the next level, I'd recommend learning more at WellnessSpringsDental.com. It's an incredible, proven, exciting dental business success concept where I know you'll come away enriched just from learning more about what we offer, let alone qualifying to participate.

I hope this book has influenced your thinking about dental success and now is the push or kick you need to rise to the greatness you know you're capable of.

Jerry A. Jones
August 1, 2014
Salem, Oregon

Made in the USA
San Bernardino, CA
26 November 2014